BioCritiques

D0068866

H

Bloom's BioCritiques

ALICE WALKER

Edited and with an introduction by
Harold Bloom
Sterling Professor of the Humanities
Yale University

CHELSEA HOUSE PUBLISHERS
Philadelphia

10 9 8 7 6 5 4 3 2

Library of Congress Cataloging-in-Publication Data

Alice Walker / edited and with an introduction by Harold Bloom.
    p. cm. – (Bloom's biocritiques)
Includes bibliographical references and index.
    ISBN 0-7910-6182-5
    1. Walker, Alice, 1944– 2. Authors, American—20th century—
Biography. 3. African-American women authors—Biography. 4. African
American authors—Biography. 5. African Americans in literature.
I. Bloom, Harold. II. Series.
    PS3573.A425 Z535 2002
    813'.54—dc21

                                        2002002188

Chelsea House Publishers
1974 Sproul Road, Suite 400
Broomall, PA 19008-0914

http://www.chelseahouse.com

Contributing editor: Heather Alumbaugh

Layout by EJB Publishing Services

CONTENTS

USER'S GUIDE

These volumes are designed to introduce the reader to the life and work of the world's literary masters. Each volume begins with Harold Bloom's essay "The Work in the Writer" and a volume-specific introduction also written by Professor Bloom. Following these unique introductions is an engaging biography that discusses the major life events and important literary accomplishments of the author under consideration.

Furthermore, each volume includes an original critique that not only traces the themes, symbols, and ideas apparent in the author's works, but strives to put those works into cultural and historical perspectives. In addition to the original critique is a brief selection of significant critical essays previously published on the author and his or her works followed by a concise and informative chronology of the writer's life. Finally, each volume concludes with a bibliography of the writer's works, a list of additional readings, and an index of important themes and ideas.

HAROLD BLOOM

The Work in the Writer

Literary biography found its masterpiece in James Boswell's *Life of Samuel Johnson*. Boswell, when he treated Johnson's writings, implicitly commented upon Johnson as found in his work, even as in the great critic's life. Modern instances of literary biography, such as Richard Ellmann's lives of W. B. Yeats, James Joyce, and Oscar Wilde, essentially follow in Boswell's pattern.

That the writer somehow is in the work, we need not doubt, though with William Shakespeare, writer-of-writers, we almost always need to rely upon pure surmise. The exquisite rancidities of the Problem Plays or Dark Comedies seem to express an extraordinary estrangement of Shakespeare from himself. When we read or attend *Troilus and Cressida* and *Measure for Measure*, we may be startled by particular speeches of Ulysses in the first play, or of Vincentio in the second. These speeches, of Ulysses upon hierarchy or upon time, or of Duke Vincentio upon death, are too strong either for their contexts or for the characters of their speakers. The same phenomenon occurs with Parolles, the military impostor of *All's Well That Ends Well*. Utterly disgraced, he nevertheless affirms: "Simply the thing I am/Shall make me live."

In Shakespeare, more even than in his peers, Dante and Cervantes, meaning always starts itself again through excess or overflow. The strongest of Shakespeare's creatures—Falstaff, Hamlet, Iago, Lear, Cleopatra—have an exuberance that is fiercer than their plays can contain. If Ben Jonson was at all correct in his complaint that "Shakespeare wanted art," it could have been only in a sense that he may not have intended. Where do the personalities of Falstaff or Hamlet touch a limit? What was it in Shakespeare that made the two parts of *Henry IV* and *Hamlet* into "plays unlimited"? Neither Falstaff nor Hamlet will be stopped: their wit, their beautiful, laughing speech, their intensity of being—all these are virtually infinite.

In what ways do Falstaff and Hamlet manifest the writer in the work? Evidently, we can never know, or know enough to answer with any authority. But what would happen if we reversed the question, and asked: How did the work form the writer, Shakespeare?

Of Shakespeare's inwardness, his biography tells us nothing. And yet, to an astonishing extent, Shakespeare created our inwardness. At the least, we can speculate that Shakespeare so lived his life as to conceal the depths of his nature, particularly as he rather prematurely aged. We do not have Shakespeare on Shakespeare, as any good reader of the Sonnets comes to realize: they do not constitute a key that unlocks his heart. No sequence of sonnets could be less confessional or more powerfully detached from the poet's self.

The German poet and universal genius, Goethe, affords a superb contrast to Shakespeare. Of Goethe's life, we know more than everything; I wonder sometimes if we know as much about Napoleon or Freud or any other human being who ever has lived, as we know about Goethe. Everywhere, we can find Goethe in his work, so much so that Goethe seems to crowd the writing out, just as Byron and Oscar Wilde seem to usurp their own literary accomplishments. Goethe, cunning beyond measure, nevertheless invested a rival exuberance in his greatest works that could match his personal charisma. The sublime outrageousness of the Second Part of *Faust*, or of the greater lyric and meditative poems, form a Counter-Sublime to Goethe's own daemonic intensity.

Goethe was fascinated by the daemonic in himself; we can doubt that Shakespeare had any such interests. Evidently, Shakespeare abandoned his acting career just before he composed *Measure for Measure* and *Othello*. I surmise that the egregious interventions by Vincentio and Iago displace the actor's energies into a new kind of mischief-making, a fresh opening to a subtler playwriting-within-the-play.

But what had opened Shakespeare to this new awareness? The answer is the work in the writer, *Hamlet* in Shakespeare. One can go further: it was not so much the play, *Hamlet*, as the character Hamlet, who changed Shakespeare's art forever.

Hamlet's personality is so large and varied that it rivals Goethe's own. Ironically Goethe's Faust, his Hamlet, has no personality at all, and is as colorless as Shakespeare himself seems to have chosen to be. Yet nothing could be more colorful than the Second Part of *Faust*, which is peopled by an astonishing array of monsters, grotesque devils, and classical ghosts.

A contrast between Shakespeare and Goethe demonstrates that in each—but in very different ways—we can better find the work in the person, than we can discover that banal entity, the person in the work. Goethe to many of his contemporaries, seemed to be a mortal god. Shakespeare, so far as we know, seemed an affable, rather ordinary fellow, who aged early and became somewhat withdrawn. Yet Faust, though Mephistopheles battles for his soul, is hardly worth the trouble unless you take him as an idea and not as a person. Hamlet is nearly every-idea-in-one, but he is precisely a personality and a person.

Would Hamlet be so astonishingly persuasive if his father's ghost did not haunt him? Falstaff is more alive than Prince Hal, who says that the devil haunts him in the shape of an old fat man. Three years before composing the final *Hamlet*, Shakespeare invented Falstaff, who then never ceased to haunt his creator. Falstaff and Hamlet may be said to best represent the work in the writer, because their influence upon Shakespeare was prodigious. W.H. Auden accurately observed that Falstaff possesses infinite energy: never tired, never bored, and absolutely both witty and happy until Hal's rejection destroys him. Hamlet too has infinite energy, but in him it is more curse than blessing.

Falstaff and Hamlet can be said to occupy the roles in Shakespeare's invented world that Sancho Panza and Don Quixote possess in Cervantes's. Shakespeare's plays from 1610 on (starting with *Twelfth Night*) are thus analogous to the Second Part of Cervantes's epic novel. Sancho and the Don overtly jostle Cervantes for authorship in the Second Part, even as Cervantes battles against the impostor who has pirated a continuation of his work. As a dramatist, Shakespeare manifests the work in the writer more indirectly. Falstaff's prose genius is revived in the scapegoating of Malvolio by Maria and Sir Toby Belch, while Falstaff's darker insights are developed by Feste's melancholic wit. Hamlet's intellectual resourcefulness, already deadly, becomes poisonous in Iago and in Edmund. Yet we have not crossed into the deeper abysses of the work in the writer in later Shakespeare.

No fictive character, before or since, is Falstaff's equal in self-trust. Sir John, whose delight in himself is contagious, has total confidence both in his self-awareness and in the resources of his language. Hamlet, whose self is as strong, and whose language is as copious, nevertheless distrusts both the self and language. Later Shakespeare is, as it were, much under the influence both of Falstaff and of Hamlet, but they tug him in opposite directions. Shakespeare's own copiousness of language is well-nigh incredible: a vocabulary in excess of twenty-one thousand words, almost eighteen hundred of which he coined himself. And of his word-hoard, nearly half are used only once each, as though the perfect setting for each had been found, and need not be repeated. Love for language and faith in language are Falstaffian attributes. Hamlet will darken both that love and that faith in Shakespeare, and perhaps the Sonnets can best be read as Falstaff and Hamlet counterpointing against one another.

Can we surmise how aware Shakespeare was of Falstaff and Hamlet, once they had played themselves into existence? *Henry IV, Part I* appeared in six quarto editions during Shakespeare's lifetime; *Hamlet* possibly had four. Falstaff and Hamlet were played again and again at the Globe, but Shakespeare knew also that they were being read, and he must have had contact with some of those readers. What would it have been like to discuss Falstaff or Hamlet with one of their early readers (presumably also part of their audience at the Globe), if you were the creator of such demiurges? The question would seem nonsensical to most Shakespeare scholars, but then these days they tend to be either ideologues or moldy figs. How can we recover the uncanniness of Falstaff and of Hamlet, when they now have become so familiar?

A writer's influence upon himself is an unexplored problem in criticism, but such an influence is never free from anxieties. The biocritical problem (which this series attempts to explore) can be divided into two areas, difficult to disengage fully. Accomplished works affect the author's life, and also affect her subsequent writings. It is simpler for me to surmise the effect of *Mrs. Dalloway* and *To the Lighthouse* upon Woolf's late *Between the Acts*, than it is to relate Clarissa Dalloway's suicide and Lily Briscoe's capable endurance in art to the tragic death and complex life of Virginia Woolf.

There are writers whose lives were so vivid that they seem sometimes to obscure the literary achievement: Byron, Wilde, Malraux, Hemingway. But most major Western writers do not live that exuberantly, and the greatest of all, Shakespeare, sometimes appears to have adopted the personal mask of colorlessness. And yet there are heroes of literature who struggled titanically with their own eras—Tolstoy, Milton, Victor Hugo—who nevertheless matter more for their works than their lives.

There are great figures—Emily Dickinson, Wallace Stevens, Willa Cather—who seem to have had so little of the full intensity of life when compared to the vitality of their work, that we might almost speak of the work in the work, rather than even of the work in a person. Emily Brontë might well be the extreme instance of such a visionary, surpassing William Blake in that one regard.

I conclude this general introduction to a series of literary bio-critiques by stating a tentative formula or principle for gauging the many ways in which the work influences the person and her subsequent, later work. Our influence upon ourselves is always related to the Shakespearean invention of self-overhearing, which I have written about in several other contexts. Life, as well as poetry and prose, is overheard rather than simply heard. The writer listens to herself as though she were somebody else, and the will to change begins to operate. The forces that live in us include the prior work we have done, and the dreams and waking visions that evade our dismissals.

HAROLD BLOOM

Introduction

At fifty-seven, Alice Walker has had a very productive literary career, the monuments of which to date are the novels *Meridian* (1976) and *The Color Purple* (1982), as well as the essays *In Search of Our Mothers' Gardens* (1983). She is a poignant rhetorician, who has found a vast audience, and has become a spokesperson for African-American feminism. Her critical admirers include the formidable bell hooks, whose defense of *The Color Purple* has a blunt eloquence:

> The tragedy embedded in the various happy endings in The Color Purple can be located at that point where fantasy triumphs over imagination, where creative power is suppressed. While this diminishes the overall aesthetic power of *The Color Purple*, it does not render meaningless those crucial moments in the text where the imagination works to liberate, to challenge, to make the new real and possible. These moments affirm the integrity of artistic vision, restore and renew.

Hooks is arguing the right use of literature for life, which is the stance Walker always refreshingly adopts when she writes about her precursor, Zora Neale Hurston. Walker's tributes to Hurston are deeply felt and strongly expressed:

> We live in a society, as blacks, women, and artists, whose contests we do not design and with whose insistence on ranking us we are permanently at war. To know that second place, in such a society, has often required more work and innate genius than first, a longer, grimmer struggle over greater odds that first—and to be

1

able to fling your scarf about dramatically while you demonstrate that you know—is to trust your own self-evaluation in the face of the Great White Western Commercial of white and male supremacy, which is virtually everything we see, outside and often inside our own homes. That Hurston held her own, literally, against the flood of whiteness and maleness that diluted so much other black art of the period in which she worked is a testimony to her genius and her faith.

As black women and as artists, we are prepared, I think, to keep that faith. There are other choices, but they are despicable. Zora Neale Hurston, who went forth into the world with one dress to her name, and who was permitted, at other times in her life, only a single pair of shoes, rescued and recreated a world which she labored to hand us whole, never underestimating the value of her gift, if at times doubting the good sense of its recipients. She appreciated us, in any case, as *we fashioned ourselves*. That is something. And of all the people in the world to be, she chose to be herself, and more *and more herself*. That, too, is something.

This is a manifesto of black female aesthetic independence, and achieves major poignance in Walker's essay "Looking for Zora":

There are times—and finding Zora Hurston's grave was one of them—when normal responses of grief, horror, and so on, do not make sense because they bear no real relation to the depth of the emotion one feels. It was impossible for me to cry when I saw the field full of weeds where Zora is. Partly this is because I have come to know Zora through her books and she was not a teary sort of person herself; but partly, too, it is because there is a point at which even grief feels absurd. And at this point, laughter gushed up to retrieve sanity.

It is only later, when the pain is not so direct a threat to one's own existence that what was learned in that moment of comical lunacy is understood. Such moments rob us of both youth and vanity. But perhaps they are also times when greater disciplines are born.

Walker's own fiction tends to move from poignance to polemic, which is sometimes an aesthetic loss. And yet there is a tenacity in her quest that compensates the reader for at least part of what is sacrificed in storytelling and in the representation of character. A didactic purpose is very difficult to sustain in fiction: it requires Tolstoyan strength to transcend the reader's sense of tendentiousness. One doesn't ask Alice Walker to be Tolstoy: by that test, no one could survive. But she frequently does take on burdens that only a Tolstoy could sustain in narrative fiction.

Walker's poems arrive at their simplicity with startling directness:

> because women are expected to keep silent about
> their close escapes I will not keep silent
> . . . .
> No I am finished with living
> for what my mother believes
> for what my brother and father defend
> for what my lover elevates
> for what my sister, blushing, denies or rushes
> to embrace

This seems to me to be Alice Walker at her most central. Whether literary criticism is relevant to this starkness, I cannot presume to say.

BRUCE & BECKY DUROST FISH

Biography of Alice Walker

THE CENTER OF CONTROVERSY

Sweltering heat, unusual for early spring, radiated from the famed red carpet as writer Alice Walker joined the line of elegantly dressed celebrities entering the Los Angeles Music Center on Monday evening, March 24, 1986. All pushed their way through an area lined by hundreds of eager fans, reporters, and photographers, all watching for their favorite film stars and directors. That night, the Hollywood elite, along with the rest of the world, would learn the names of those judged the year's best film artists at the 58th annual Academy Awards.

Among the films under consideration was *The Color Purple*, directed by Steven Spielberg and based on Walker's award-winning novel of the same title. The movie had been nominated in 11 categories, and many observers believed it was certain to receive at least a few of the coveted Oscars before the night was over.

But like Alice Walker, *The Color Purple* stirred up controversy. As Alice approached the main entrance to the music center, she noticed signs supporting Steven Spielberg, who, despite being named best director by the Directors' Guild of America earlier that month, hadn't been nominated by the Academy of Motion Picture Arts and Sciences. "Hey, Oscar, you're losing credibility" and "Spielberg's Been Oscardized" read some of the signs.

Walker also noticed many African-American picketers demonstrating against *The Color Purple*. Organized primarily by the Coalition Against Black Exploitation, the protestors shouted slogans and held signs objecting to the movie's negative portrayal of African-American men. "Going into the theater

I had a buoyant sense of what battered and burnished warriors we were," Walker later wrote. "By then I knew that almost everyone making the movie had done it, like me, against a personal backdrop of suffering and stress. Marriages were failing, affairs were coming apart, money was tight, physical ailments abounded, households were coming unglued, friendships disengaged. Still, like Celie [the main character in *The Color Purple*], we were there. I felt, simply, that the people arrayed against us, shouting or glaring angrily, were wrong, and that time would prove them so." [*The Same River Twice*, p. 285]

But that proof would not come from the Academy. One by one, as the winners were announced, a growing sense of disbelief swept through the auditorium. By the time the producers of *Out of Africa* stepped forward to receive the Oscar for Best Picture, stunned supporters of *The Color Purple* realized that their movie, with its 11 nominations, had won not a single Academy Award.

The results of the Oscar voting created almost as much controversy as *The Color Purple* itself. As Dorothy Gillia observed in a *Washington Post* article later that week, "Because other strong black films that were Oscar contenders have been shut out in the past, Hollywood's historical racism is also a factor here. In the Academy's history, only three black actors have won Oscars, and all for work with predominantly white casts." The Hollywood–Beverly Hills branch of the National Association for the Advancement of Colored People (NAACP) sent a formal letter of protest to the Academy. Radio station WDJY in Washington, D.C. encouraged listeners to wear a purple ribbon in protest. "I think there is a very strong social implication," said the film's music composer and also one of its producers, Quincy Jones, after the ceremony. Gillia concluded, "That's the way it is, and we'll have to do something about it."

Alice Walker herself had a slightly different take on the controversy. "Because I know that some of our people wanted awards, for whatever reason," she wrote 10 years later, "I said nothing about how relieved I was that *The Color Purple* did not receive any. It isn't just that I did not know a single soul making decisions on behalf of the Academy, it was that I was aware of the kind of black characters who had been anointed before. Maids and other white family retainers." [*Same River*, p. 285]

This opinion was reinforced by her opinion of the film that received the most awards, *Out of Africa*. "For me, not getting an award for *The Color Purple*, especially after so many nominations, felt very clean," she wrote.

> *Out of Africa* is reactionary and racist. It glamorizes the rape of
> Africa and attempts to make colonialists look like saviors. . . . It
> patronizes black people shockingly, and its sly, gratuitous
> denigration of the black woman is insufferable. But it is a

worldview the Academy understood, and upheld. Some black people, outraged that one black woman in *The Color Purple* might physically express her love for another, let [the offensive material in *Out of Africa*] go by without a murmur, as they let go by film after film, decade after decade, by black directors and white, in which women and people of color are insulted, randomly trashed, raped, battered, brutalized and murdered. [*Same River*, p. 286]

Such a blunt appraisal is typical of Alice Walker, who has used her gifts as a writer and as a speaker to motivate action. Throughout her adult life, Walker has fought for justice and equality, not concerning herself with the "politically correct." In the process, she has earned some of the world's most prestigious writing awards. Yet the seeds of both her activism and her literary talent were planted in a small Southern town: Eatonton, Georgia.

ALTERED VISION

In 1944, Eatonton, Georgia resembled many other small rural communities in the Deep South. Most of its young men were in Europe or the South Pacific, fighting in World War II. Black and white children attended separate schools. The window of a local restaurant proudly displayed a dummy of an elderly black man seated in a rocking chair; it was meant to represent Uncle Remus, a fictional slave created by white writer Joel Chandler Harris, who had lived in Eatonton. African Americans were not allowed to patronize the restaurant.

As the year began, Willie Lee Walker and his wife, Minnie Tallulah (Grant) Walker, struggled to hold together their family of seven children. Like most of his black neighbors, Willie Lee worked on a dairy farm and as a sharecropper. He raised crops on another man's land in exchange for a small percentage of the money earned from the harvest. By the time charges for seed, tools, living quarters, and food were deducted from those earnings, he was left with only $300 a year, approximately, provided that bad weather or disease didn't destroy the crops.

Willie's wife Minnie worked part-time as a maid and brought home even less money than he did. When at home, she worked in the fields with Willie Lee and made all the clothing for her family, as well as the towels and sheets they used. During the summer, she canned fruit and vegetables for use during the winter, and when cold weather arrived, she made quilts to keep her family warm.

Throughout the winter of 1944, Willie Lee and Minnie Walker prepared for the birth of their unplanned eighth child; on February 9, the baby arrived. The Walkers called in a midwife to help with this delivery, just as they had done when their other seven children had been born, and would pay her in kind —a pig, a quilt, or jars of canned fruits and vegetables—for her services. The Walkers named their little girl Alice. The new baby quickly blended in with the rest of the family. Her older brothers and sisters helped to look out for her, and she quickly grew into an active toddler.

When Alice was about three years old, she accidentally broke a fruit jar. Used for canning fruit, such jars were very valuable to the Walkers, and they could not afford to buy new ones. When her father asked her if she knew anything about the broken jar, the little girl did not know whether he knew she was guilty. She could lie, and risk a whipping for her lie, or she could tell the truth and risk a whipping for breaking the jar. She sensed that what her father really wanted was that she tell the truth, and when she did so he hugged her. "I think it was at that moment that I resolved to take my chances with the truth," she later wrote, "although as the years rolled on I was to break more serious things in his scheme of things than fruit jars." [*Living by the Word: Selected Writings 1973–1987*, p. 12]

A precocious child, Alice came to the attention of one of her teachers when she was only four years old. The woman was struck by Alice's intelligence and, having replaced Alice's ragged clothing, established the girl in the first grade. One of Alice Walker's earliest memories from school is of reciting memorized poems and stories. She stood before the class wearing an organdy dress, white anklets, and patent leather shoes. "I always tried to give it flourish," she explained later in a 1989 interview with *Life*. She gave similar recitations during services at the church her family attended.

Much of Walker's ability to give poised public recitations grew out of the lessons in storytelling she received from her parents, who were extremely gifted in this area. Many evenings, the elder Walkers gathered their children around the fireplace or on the front porch and told African folk tales that had been passed down in their family for generations. Stories about Brer Rabbit and Brer Fox captivated young Alice's imagination, and she often heard them repeated by her grandparents and other relatives who lived in the area. The Walkers also told their children about their ancestors, one of whom, a woman by the name of Mary Poole, had reportedly lived from approximately 1800 until 1921. While a slave, Mary Poole had been forced to walk from Virginia to Georgia, carrying two young children. Alice was struck by her great-grandmother's strength, dignity, and longevity.

But some of the stories confused Alice. She often heard about how her father had organized a group of black men in the 1930s to vote in Eatonton. No black man had ever voted in the town before, and doing so put their lives in danger. Most of their white employers did not want black men voting, and lynchings were still fairly common in the South. Alice also was told about how her father became one of the leading supporters of the local one-room black school. But this image of Willie Lee Walker differed from the man Alice knew, almost always sick from a combination of hypertension and diabetes. His illnesses did not keep him bedridden—or perhaps, as Alice later speculated, with so many children to support he could not afford to lie down—but it was obvious that he had little energy.

Willie Lee Walker's attitudes toward politics and education, too, appeared to have changed since those fabled days. "He seemed fearful of both education and politics and disappointed and resentful as well," Alice recalled. [*Living*, p. 13] As an adult, she attributed this change to disillusionment from years of fighting a system that refused to change, but as a child she could not understand how one man's views could alter so dramatically.

Minnie Walker, however, still strongly argued the need for a good education. Alice only remembers her mother becoming extremely angry on those occasions when their white landlord remarked that black children did not need to go to school.

By the time she was eight years old, Alice's family knew she would rather play more exciting games with two of her older brothers than spend her time with dolls. The children often acted out stories from the Westerns their mother loved to watch at the local theater. Once, while they were playing, Alice suddenly felt a blow to her right eye; one of her brothers had shot her with his BB gun. The two boys begged Alice to tell their parents that she had stepped on a long piece of wire and that the other end had popped up and hit her in the eye. Otherwise, her brothers worried, they would be whipped. She agreed to the plan, and they went to their parents, who placed Alice on a bench on the front porch and examined the injury.

The last thing Alice saw out of her right eye was a tree growing near the porch. She remembers watching its trunk, its branches, and finally its leaves disappear as blood obscured her vision. Her eye was permanently blinded, and an ugly mass of white scar tissue formed over it. Later she learned that her father had stood by the road, trying to flag down a car so that they could take her to a doctor and that a white man had at first stopped but, on learning what was needed, had driven away, apparently unwilling to inconvenience himself for a black child.

Suddenly, Alice no longer saw herself as a pretty little girl. Her family had recently moved to a home across the county line, so she had to attend another school. She didn't know any of the other students, and she refused to look at them because she was ashamed of her appearance. The other children constantly teased her about her injured eye, and some of them picked fights with her. Her grades plummeted, and she was obviously miserable. After several months, her parents sent Alice to live with her grandparents, that she might be schooled with her former friends. But the eight-year-old Alice still felt ugly, and almost every night she looked into a mirror and yelled at her eye, telling it how much she hated it. Rather than praying for sight, she prayed for beauty.

Afraid of interacting with other children and adults, Alice began to spend more and more time reading, writing poetry, and quietly observing the people around her. One of these people was an old guitar player named Mr. Sweet, who used to play his "box," as he called his instrument, while sitting in the kitchen of Alice's grandmother. Sounds of the blues filled the cozy room. "I know that Mr. Sweet was a fixture, a rare and honored presence in our family," Alice later wrote, "and we were taught to respect him—no matter that he drank, loved to gamble and shoot off his gun, and went 'crazy' several times a year. He was an artist. He went deep into his own pain and brought out words and music that made us happy, made us feel empathy for anyone in trouble, made us think. We were taught to be thankful that anyone would assume this risk." [*Living*, p. 38]

After living with her grandparents for a year, Alice returned to her parents' home, but she still struggled with feelings of inferiority. Her world received yet another jolt in 1956, shortly after Walt Disney Studios reissued its film *Song of the South*. The film was an adaptation of the Uncle Remus stories that Joel Chandler Harris had written in the 1880s and which had since become immensely popular among white children; these were based on tales Harris and other white children had heard slaves recount to their own children in the 1850s and 1860s on the Eatonton plantation on which Harris had lived.

Because Harris had lived in Eatonton, which boasted even a museum about him, the whole town turned out to see *Song of the South* at the local theater. The Walkers and their children sat with their neighbors in the black section of the theater, in the balcony. White families sat in the better seats below.

As the movie played and Alice saw the characters of Brer Rabbit and Brer Fox appear on the screen, she was stunned. The 12-year-old girl had had no idea that Harris's books were based on the stories she'd heard from her parents since she was very young. She later explained how the movie made her feel ashamed of her heritage:

> I experienced [the movie] as vastly alienating, not only from the likes of Uncle Remus—in whom I saw aspects of my father, my mother, in fact all black people I knew who told these stories— but also from the stories themselves, which, passed into the context of white people's creation . . . I perceived as meaningless. So there I was, at an early age, separated from my own folk culture by an invention.

I believe that the worst part of being in an oppressed culture is that the oppressive culture—primarily because it controls the production and dispersal of images in the media—can so easily make us feel ashamed of ourselves, of our sayings, our doings, and our ways. [*Living*, pp. 31–32]

At the age of 14, Alice traveled to Boston to care for the family of her married older brother, Bill. Bill and his wife paid a doctor to remove the white cataract from Alice's right eye. The eye, still blind, now held a bluish crater, but the change in her appearance transformed Alice. For the first time in six years, Alice held her head high and looked people straight in the eye. When she returned to Eatonton, she made many friends and her grades improved dramatically.

As she grew older, Alice saw, through her first boyfriend, a new facet of her father's character. Willie Lee Walker set extremely strict dating standards for all his daughters, in part because his own mother had been shot and killed on the way home from church by a man whose attentions she had spurned. He was particularly hard on one of Alice's older sisters because the girl looked so much like his murdered mother. Alice hated to see such unfair treatment, but she was powerless to change her father's ways.

Her intolerance of injustice extended to other areas as well. Once, while her boyfriend, Porter Sanford III, was driving Alice and another student to their summer jobs, Alice talked of the unfairness of their having to walk to school while the white children had a school bus. She also complained their white counterparts were paid more for doing the same work Alice and her friends did. Porter made the mistake of saying that they just had to accept the situation. "Alice got so mad at me that she demanded to be let out of the car," he recalled years later. "And she dragged the other guy out with her. It must have been five or six miles, but she walked the rest of the way to work. She was always real serious about her issues." ["Alice Walker on Activism," by Evelyn C. White, *Black Collegian*, October 1997]

Those issues were enlarged in 1960 with Minnie Walker's purchase of a battered television set. Every day after school, Alice watched reports of two black students struggling to integrate the University of Georgia. Then, one day, Alice saw the face of Martin Luther King Jr. appear on the screen. The civil rights leader was being handcuffed and forced into a police truck, but he exuded a sense of peace. "At the moment I saw his resistance I knew I would never be able to live in this country without resisting everything that sought to disinherit me," Alice later wrote, "and I would never be forced away from the land of my birth without a fight." [*In Search of Our Mothers' Gardens*, p. 144]

In 1961, Alice Walker graduated from high school as valedictorian of her class, and her classmates voted her most popular student. Her one memory from the graduation ceremony was the commencement speech, given by Mr. Bullock, a well-known horticulturalist from Atlanta. He mentioned that Coca-Cola had been invented by a black woman. "Everybody snapped awake," Alice wrote in a later essay. "For didn't most of us drink this part of our heritage every day?" [*Living*, p. 102]

Alice added the bit of information about Coca-Cola to the collection of stories, both real and fictional, she had gathered throughout her childhood. Armed with this knowledge and a well-developed sense of justice, Alice Walker stood ready to enter the larger world. Her next home would be Spelman College in Atlanta.

DISCOVERING A LARGER WORLD

Late in the summer of 1961, Alice Walker stood at a bus depot, waiting for the ride that would take her to Atlanta, Georgia, about 75 miles west-northwest of Eatonton. Because she was valedictorian of her class and was blind in her right eye, Alice had qualified for a scholarship from the state. Black neighbors and family members had collected $75 to cover the cost of the bus ticket and provide some "pocket money" for her first year at Spelman.

Alice also carried three special gifts from her mother, who had carefully saved for them from her $20-a-week salary as a maid. Walker later said that each of the gifts had imparted an important message: a sewing machine, so that Alice could make her own clothes, signifying self-sufficiency and independence; a high-quality leather suitcase, symbolizing the freedom to travel the world and to come home whenever she needed to; and a typewriter, for the recording of not only her own stories, but also those of her mother.

Although her mother encouraged Alice's further education, her father seemed ambivalent. "My father stood outside the bus that day," Alice wrote years later, "his hat—an old gray fedora—in his hands, helpless as I left the only world he would ever know. . . . So we never spoke of this parting, or of the pain in his beautiful eyes as the bus left him there by the side of that lonely Georgia highway, and I moved—blinded by tears of guilt and relief—ever farther and farther away." ["My Father's Country Is the Poor," *New York Times*, 21 March 1977]

When she boarded the bus, Walker sat near the front, something black people were not permitted to do in Georgia at that time. A white woman complained to the bus driver, who ordered Walker to move. She complied, but her determination remained. "Even as I moved, in confusion and anger and tears, I knew he had not seen the last of me," Walker wrote later. ["Staying Home in Mississippi, *New York Times*, 26 August 1973]

Walker quickly settled into life at Spelman College. Historically for black women, Spelman was founded in the basement of an Atlanta church in 1881 by two women from Boston who taught 10 black women and one black girl—mostly former slaves. By 1961, in part because of financial support from the Rockefeller family, it had expanded into a highly regarded college. For the first time in her life, Walker was exposed to black women of her own age who were interested in issues of racial equality and intellectual growth.

Soon Walker became involved in the weekly civil rights demonstrations held on Saturday mornings in downtown Atlanta, where she heard speeches given by civil rights leaders such as John Lewis and Julian Bond. With other students, she participated in sit-ins at Atlanta's segregated lunch counters. Following the nonviolent protest methods developed by Mahatma Gandhi, the students would sit in the "whites only" section of the lunch counter until forcibly removed by police officers. The brutality often used in these forced removals gained sympathy for the cause of civil rights.

In the summer of 1962, after her freshman year of college, Walker was among a group of Spelman students, sponsored by African-American churches, who attended the Youth World Peace Festival in Helsinki, Finland. Before they left for Europe, the group's advisor arranged for them to meet Coretta Scott King. Mrs. King and her husband, civil rights leader Martin Luther King Jr., lived in a modest house a few blocks from the Spelman campus. "As she talked briefly to us," Walker later recalled, "I sat on the sofa and stared at her, much too shy myself to speak. I was satisfied just to witness her exuberance, her brightness, her sparkle and smiles, as she talked about the peace movement, her music, and all her plans." [*Our Mothers' Gardens*, p. 147]

After the conference in Helsinki, Walker toured other parts of Europe, relishing the opportunity to experience different cultures and meet new people. When she returned to Spelman that fall, she balanced her time between a busy studying schedule and immersion in civil rights activities.

The next summer, Walker took a job in Boston, where she lived with an older brother and other relatives, and earned more money for her next year of college than she would have been possible in Eatonton. But a temporary absence from Georgia did not mean she would neglect her involvement in the Civil Rights Movement. Before dawn on August 28, 1963, Walker joined a boisterous crowd singing "We Shall Overcome" as they boarded a bus headed for Washington, D.C. On arrival, they joined an interracial gathering of more than 200,000 people who stood in the shadow of the Lincoln Memorial, demanding freedom and justice for all Americans. As part of this historic March on Washington, Martin Luther King Jr. gave his famous "I Have a Dream" speech, in which he graphically described the injustices that existed in American society toward African Americans and revealed a compelling vision of what America could be if truly there were liberty and justice for all.

Walker's Boston relatives watched television coverage of the event and claimed that they had seen someone who looked exactly like her in the crowd to the left of Dr. King. "But of course I was not anywhere near him," Walker later reported. "The crowds would not allow it. I was, instead, perched on the limb of a tree far from the Lincoln Memorial, and although I managed to see very little of the speakers, I could hear everything." [*Our Mothers' Gardens*, pp. 158–59] The words she heard steeled her resolve. "When [King] spoke of 'letting freedom ring' across 'the green hills of Alabama and the red hills of Georgia' I saw again what he was always uniquely able to make me see: that I, in fact, had claim to the land of my birth. Those red hills of Georgia were mine, and nobody was going to force me away from them until I myself was good and ready to go." [*Our Mother's Gardens*, p. 160]

When Walker returned to Spelman College that fall as a junior, however, she was ready for change. While she thrived on her involvement with civil rights groups such as the Student Nonviolent Coordinating Committee, she felt that the Spelman administration did not support her activism. She later described Spelman as "a school that I considered opposed to change, to freedom, and to understanding that by the time most girls enter college they are already women and should be treated as women." [*Our Mothers' Gardens*, p. 130] When the prestigious Sarah Lawrence College, in Bronxville, New York, offered her a scholarship, she gladly accepted, transferring during her junior year.

Bronxville is only a few miles north of the Bronx (one of the boroughs of New York City), but it embodies a completely different world. Hilly and green, filled with homes in the Tudor, colonial, and Victorian styles, it represents the antithesis of urban life. Sarah Lawrence College is located on a 35-acre campus designed to look like a rural English village. When Walker arrived in Bronxville, only female students attended Sarah Lawrence. Each student was assigned a don, or faculty advisor, with whom to design a course of study.

Walker's don was Helen Merrell Lynd, who Walker later said was the first person she'd met who made philosophy understandable. "It was she who led me through the works of Camus," Walker said while speaking at Sarah Lawrence seven years after her graduation, "and showed me, for the first time, how life and suffering are always teachers, or, as with Camus, life and suffering, *and* joy. Like Rilke, I came to understand that even loneliness has a use, and that sadness is positively the wellspring of creativity. Since studying with her, all of life, the sadness as well as the joy, has its magnificence, its meaning, and its *use*." [*Our Mothers' Gardens*, p. 38]

Some of the sadness Walker herself experienced resulted from feeling somewhat out of place at Sarah Lawrence. She described it as "an environment so different from the one in which . . . I had been brought up, that it might have existed on another planet. There were only three or four other black people there, and no poor people at all as far as the eye could see." [*Living*, p. 38] More than 20 years after she graduated from college, she told an interviewer, "It was a dreadful time—a posh outpost in hell." ["Alice Walker's Soul-Saving Story," by John M. Leighty, UPI, 3 June 1988]

The repercussions of a trip to Africa during the summer between her junior and senior years of college brought further pain. Before the end of the fall semester, Walker discovered she was pregnant; a development that she knew would disappoint and shame her parents. She contemplated suicide and even slept with a razor blade under her pillow. Through a friend, Walker made contact with a doctor who was willing to perform what was then an illegal abortion. She underwent the procedure, but her depression and suicidal feelings did not subside.

It was also around this time that Walker learned that Mr. Sweet, the old guitar player from her childhood, had died. Looking at his life from an adult perspective, she began to recognize the magnitude of the problems he had faced as a black artist, living in poverty and facing violent racism. She reached an important conclusion about his life: "*Irregardless,* as the old people said . . . not only had he lived to a ripe old age . . . but he had continued to share all his troubles and his insights with anyone who would listen, taking special care to craft them for the necessary effect. *He continued to sing.*" [*Living*, p. 39]

"Turning my back on the razor blade," Walker continued, "I went to a friend's house for the Christmas holidays (I was too poor even to consider making the trip home, a distance of about a thousand miles), and on the day of Mr. Sweet's burial I wrote 'To Hell with Dying.'" [*Living*, p. 39] The short story is about the love of a young girl for a dying old man and is based to some degree on her relationships with her grandfathers.

During her last semester in college, Walker entered a period of intense creativity, and her depression lifted. She began to write poetry seriously and showed her work to the poet Muriel Rukeyser and to Jane Cooper, the teacher of a writing course Walker was taking—both were teachers at Sarah Lawrence who had influenced Walker greatly. The two women were impressed with their student's work and urged her to continue writing. Rukeyser sent a copy of "To Hell with Dying" to the great African-American poet Langston Hughes, who sent to Alice a hand-written note of encouragement. Rukeyser also put the collection of poems into the hands of her own literary agent, Monica McCall. Both actions laid the foundation for Walker's future success.

In 1965, Walker graduated from Sarah Lawrence College with a Bachelor of Arts degree. The world seemed to be filled with possibilities—

but she would first return to Georgia, where she would continue her personal fight for justice.

The Political Activist

Political activism took center stage in Alice Walker's life when she returned to Georgia in the summer of 1965. The Civil Rights Act had become law the previous year, guaranteeing equal voting rights to all U.S. citizens. It outlawed voter registration requirements that had been used in many Southern states to keep minorities and the poor from voting. In part because of this new law, many civil rights groups launched huge voter registration drives. Going from door to door in Liberty County, Georgia, Walker registered voters among the rural, predominantly African-American poor.

Part of the reason Walker returned to Georgia was the challenge she had repeatedly heard Martin Luther King Jr. issue to African Americans: "Go back to Mississippi, go back to Alabama, go back . . . to Georgia . . . knowing that somehow this situation can and will be changed." ["Staying Home in Mississippi"] Eighteen years later, Walker would describe her reasons for returning to Georgia: "I went back to Georgia . . . in general looking at the South to see if it was worth claiming. I suppose I decided it *was* worth something." ["Staying Home in Mississippi"] And although she had not planned on it, her exposure to the poorest people in the state gave her an opportunity to see how poverty affected the relationships between black men and women, an issue that would appear often in her writing.

During the summer, Walker received exciting news about the group of her poems that Muriel Rukeyser had passed on to her own agent. Harcourt Publishing editor Hiram Haydn had accepted the collection of poems, under the title *Once*. It would not be published immediately, but just knowing her work would appear as a book encouraged the young writer.

That fall, Walker returned to New York City. "I went to work for the New York City Welfare Department to support my writing, living on the Lower East Side between Avenue A and Avenue B in a building that had no front door," she later explained in an interview. "I'm not at all nostalgic for the place. I remained with the Welfare Department for four months, writing at night, but I couldn't stand it." ["Alice Walker Recalls the Civil Rights Battle," by Herbert Mitgang, *New York Times*, 16 April 1983]

With the new year came new opportunities. Walker won a writing fellowship from the prestigious Bread Loaf Writers' Conference in Ripton, Vermont. She had also planned to go to Senegal, West Africa, but instead she flew to Mississippi to continue work in the Civil Rights Movement. "That summer marked the beginning of a realization that I could never live happily in Africa—or anywhere else—until I could live freely in Mississippi," Walker later wrote. ["Staying Home in Mississippi"]

She also wanted to be able to *choose* to live in the South, where she had been raised. White writers from the South, such as William Faulkner, Eudora Welty, and Flannery O'Connor, had felt free to live where they had been born, but Walker believed that African-American writers such as Richard Wright had not had such a choice because of the racism and physical dangers they faced. "Black writers have generally left the South as soon as possible," she observed. "The strain of creation and constant exposure to petty insults and legally encouraged humiliations proved too great. But their departure impoverished those they left behind." ["Staying Home in Mississippi"]

While working in Mississippi, Walker met a young white Jewish law student named Melvyn Leventhal. The two fell in love, but the sight of a white man dating a black woman angered some white southerners. One night, Walker and Leventhal went swimming in the Ross Barnett Reservoir in Jackson, Mississippi, a recreational area named for the Mississippi governor who had opposed integrating the University of Mississippi. State troopers descended on the couple with suspicion. On another day, in Greenwood, Mississippi, a man approached Walker in the motel in which she was staying and warned, "Don't you let the sun go down on you in this here town." Taking the hint, she asked some of her civil rights colleagues to escort her from Greenwood before sunset. ["Alice Walker Recalls the Civil Rights Battle"]

That fall, she returned to New York City with Leventhal, where they lived together in one room above Washington Square Park. Their parents and many of their friends were not happy with the living arrangement. Finances were tight for the law student and writer, so they were thrilled when Walker won the annual essay contest sponsored by *The American Scholar*. "The Civil Rights Movement: What Good Was It?" was her first essay to see publication and earned her $300 in prize money. "The money was almost magically reassuring to us in those days of disaffected parents, outraged friends, and one-item meals, and kept us in tulips, peonies, daisies, and lamb chops for several months," Walker later recounted. [*Our Mothers' Gardens*, p. 119]

In her essay, Walker took issue with the view of many white civil rights activists that the movement was dead because of increasing violence, political gains by conservatives, and dissension within the movement itself. She argued that the Civil Rights Movement was dead only to the white man. "He can take a rest from the news of beatings, killings, and arrests that reach him from North and South—if his skin is white. Negroes cannot now and will never be able to take a rest from the injustices that plague them, for they—not the white man—are the target." [*Our Mothers' Gardens*, p. 121] She then she stated that, even if the movement *was* dead, it already had justified its existence:

If the Civil Rights Movement is "dead," and if it gave us nothing else, it gave us each other forever. . . . It gave us our children, our husbands, our brothers, our fathers, as men reborn and with a purpose for living. It broke the pattern of black servitude in this country. It shattered the phony "promise" of white soap operas that sucked away so many pitiful lives. . . . It gave us heroes, selfless men of courage and strength, for our little boys and girls to follow. It gave us hope for tomorrow. It called us to life.

Because we live, it can never die. [*Our Mothers' Gardens*, pp. 128–29]

Encouraged by winning the essay contest, Walker applied for and won a writing fellowship at the highly regarded MacDowell Colony in Peterborough, New Hampshire. She also received the Merrill writing fellowship, and the money that came with this award enabled her to devote more of her time to the writing of a novel. Langston Hughes included "To Hell with Dying," which he had first seen while she was still in college, in an anthology he edited, *The Best Short Stories by Negro Writers from 1899 to the Present* (1967).

During this time, Leventhal was finishing law school in New York and planned to return to Mississippi to work on civil rights cases with the NAACP. Walker saw in Leventhal a man who both encouraged her writing and shared her passion for justice and equal rights; they were married on March 17, 1967.

While living in New York City, Walker had met Langston Hughes several times and had introduced him to her future husband. When Walker and Leventhal were married, Hughes sent her a note which said, in part, "You married your subsidy." [*The Way Forward Is with a Broken Heart*, p. 15] Walker later wrote that she had been too young at the time to understand the allusion to the white men and women who had subsidized Hughes' early career, and it left her with unanswered questions that she later asked in an essay addressed to Leventhal: "Did you remind Langston of these men? And did our relationship remind him of relationships he had known? And was he saying I did not love you? Or that love was only part of it?" [*The Way Forward*, p. 16]

Langston Hughes never heard those questions, though; he died on May 22, 1967, some thirty-three years before their publication. Walker and Leventhal attended the funeral, which, according to an analysis Walker later addressed to Leventhal, evolved into a party:

Like him, [the funeral] turned us back on ourselves, while being superbly—with its lively music and energetic poetry reading—entertaining. At this "celebration" and for years afterward I thought of his words, especially as you, unfailingly generous, supported me, supported my work. Read it, critiqued it, praised it, ran off multiple copies of it on the big Xerox machine in your law office. Sat in the audience wherever I read it with the biggest glow of all on your face. I had never experienced such faith before. [*The Way Forward*, p. 16]

That summer, the couple moved to Mississippi, where Leventhal worked on court cases aimed at desegregating public schools in Jackson. Walker became a teacher with the local Head Start program. In part, they hoped that relocating would help them to escape the reminders of family rejection. When Minnie Walker first met Leventhal, she had said, referring to his Jewish heritage, "You're one of the ones that killed Christ." [*Same River*, p. 168], and when Leventhal's mother learned that her son had married a black woman, she first stormed their New York City apartment to remove all clothing that she had given to him, then told other family members not to speak to him, and finally sat shiva, a seven-day Jewish observance of mourning for the dead, for her living son.

Leventhal and Walker were hopeful about their future together, however, and soon found even greater cause for celebration: Walker discovered that she was pregnant. Not only were she and Leventhal looking forward to being parents, but fatherhood would excuse Leventhal from being drafted into military service in the Vietnam War, a circumstance all the more fortunate now that he no longer qualified for educational deferments.

Walker and Leventhal were among the first legally married interracial couples to live in Mississippi, where, at the time, it was illegal for interracial couples to *be* married. While Walker's ethnicity and Leventhal's Jewish heritage and civil rights activities would have been enough to make them targets of hatred in Mississippi at that time, their status as a couple heightened the dangers they faced. Four years earlier, in June of 1963, NAACP leader Medgar Evers had been shot and killed in his driveway. In the following year, the Ku Klux Klan, drawing national attention when they killed a trio of civil rights workers. Mississippi officials refused to prosecute any of the men implicated in the murders. Then in 1967, the same year Walker and Leventhal moved to Mississippi, a 36-year-old NAACP officer from Natchez was killed when a bomb exploded in his truck.

Both Walker and Leventhal were threatened. They lived with a guard dog, slept with a gun under their bed for protection, and kept the doors to their rented home bolted. Neighbors called to warn them whenever a car full of white strangers cruised the streets, afraid that the strangers might be planning an attack on the couple.

In October of 1967, eighteen people were brought to trial in federal court, charged by the federal government with violating the civil rights of the three men who had been killed in 1964. Seven of the accused were found guilty and sentenced to prison terms ranging from three to ten years. In part because of the national attention the trial received, and perhaps because one of the civil rights workers slain was a Jewish man from New York, Leventhal's mother decided to resurrect her relationship with her son and his wife. "She began to think," Alice later explained, "killing her son figuratively was a bad idea, since there were so many people in the world, and especially in Mississippi, who would happily do it literally. She came South, in obvious pain, to embrace her son and to attempt to tolerate me." [*Same River*, p. 169]

On April 4, 1968, Martin Luther King Jr. was shot and killed while standing on a balcony of the Lorraine Motel in Memphis, Tennessee. The news devastated Walker. She and Leventhal traveled to Atlanta to attend King's funeral services at Ebenezer Baptist Church and on the campus of Morehouse College, held on April 9. Walker was impressed by the apparent calm of King's widow, Coretta Scott King, whom she had not seen since the 1962 meeting at the Kings' home, when Walker had still been a student at Spelman College.

A week after King's funeral, Walker suffered a miscarriage. "I did not even care," she wrote in an article for *Redbook* three years later:

> It seemed to me, at the time, that if "he" (it was weeks before my tongue could form his name) must die no one deserved to live, not even my own child. I thought, as I lay on my bed listening to the rude Mississippi accents around me, that with any luck I could lose myself. I do not recall wanting very much to live. A week later, however, I saw Coretta's face again, on television, and perhaps it was my imagination, but she sounded so much like her husband that for a minute I thought I was hearing his voice. . . .
>
> I knew then that my grief was really self-pity; something I don't believe either Martin or Coretta had time to feel. I was still angry, confused, and, unlike Coretta, I have wandered very far, I think, from my belief in God if not from my faith in humanity, but she pulled me to my feet, as her husband had done in a different way, and forced me to acknowledge the debt I owed, not only to her husband's memory but also to the living continuation of his work. [*Our Mothers' Gardens*, p. 148]

To this end, Walker continued to teach at Head Start and became a writer in residence and a teacher of black studies at Jackson State College. That same year, *Once: Poems*, her first collection of poetry, which had been contracted to Harcourt Publishing three years earlier, was released. Walker also continued work on her first novel, *The Third Life of Grange Copeland*, which was funded partly by a 1969 grant from the National Endowment for the Arts.

Copeland drew on observations Walker had made while working with extremely poor families in rural Mississippi. She had seen many examples of how poverty destroyed relationships between black men and women, and that knowledge informed her characters. The novel tells the story of Grange Copeland, a man who abuses his young wife and son and then abandons them to find a more prosperous life in the North. Years later he returns to find his adult son abusing his own family. Eventually, that son murders his wife, after leaving their newborn daughter on a porch to freeze to death. Copeland determines he will rescue his granddaughter and teach her how to protect herself both from her abusive father and from white people. Through that process, he himself is redeemed.

Walker's discovery of her second pregnancy made the writing of *Copeland* into a race against time. She finished the novel on November 14, 1969, three days before the birth of her daughter, Rebecca. Minnie Walker marked the birth by giving to Alice a cutting from an old-fashioned petunia she had maintained for 37 years, transplanting it each time the family had moved. Alice saw this flower as a heritage, reflecting her mother's own ability to survive, no matter what circumstances she faced.

Walker found the task of balancing her writing with the care of an infant challenging. "I wrote nothing for a year that didn't sound as though a baby were screaming right through the middle of it," she once told another writer. [*Our Mothers' Gardens*, p. 66] But she persevered all the same. In 1970, Walker's research led her to discover the work of an earlier African-American writer, and the discovery would radically change her life.

SPEAKING HER MIND

Late in 1970, Alice Walker was researching the voodoo practices of African Americans in the rural South during the 1930s for her short story "The Revenge of Hannah Kemhuff." "A number of white, racist anthropologists and folklorists of the period had, not surprisingly, disappointed and insulted me," Walker later wrote. "They thought blacks inferior, peculiar, and comic, and for me this undermined, no, *destroyed*, the relevance of their books. Fortunately, it was then that I discovered *Mules and Men*, Zora's book on folklore, collecting, herself, and her small, all-black community in Eatonville, Florida." [*Our Mothers' Gardens*, p. 83]

Zora Neale Hurston, to whom Walker was referring, was an African-American writer who was born in Alabama in 1891 and raised in Eatonville, Florida, historically recognized as the first incorporated all-black municipality in the nation. Educated at Howard University, Barnard College, and Columbia University, Hurston combined her training in anthropology with her knowledge of African-American folklore and traditions to create a body of highly regarded fiction and nonfiction. When she died penniless in 1960, her work was largely forgotten until the late 20th century.

Walker fell in love with Hurston's writings. She read excerpts from *Mules and Men* to her relatives and reported:

> no matter how much distance they tried to maintain between themselves, as new sophisticates, and the lives their parents and grandparents lived, no matter how they tried to remain cool toward all Zora revealed, in the end they could not hold back the smiles, the laughter, the joy over who she was showing them to be: descendants of an inventive, joyous, courageous, and outrageous people; loving drama, appreciating wit, and, most of all, relishing the pleasure of each other's loquacious and *bodacious* company. [*Our Mothers' Gardens*, p. 85]

But Walker also made a disturbing discovery. Having been captivated by Hurston's works, which she felt portrayed African Americans as complex individuals rather than as stereotypical characters, she wanted to know what other people had written about her. Walker's discoveries traumatized her:

> After reading the misleading, deliberately belittling, inaccurate, and generally irresponsible attacks on her work and her life by almost everyone, I became for a time paralyzed with confusion and fear," Walker wrote. "For if a woman who had given so much of obvious value to all of us (and at such risks: to health, reputation, sanity) could be so casually pilloried and consigned to a sneering oblivion, what chance would someone else—for example, myself—have? I was aware that I had much less gumption than Zora. [*Our Mothers' Gardens*, pp. 86–87]

Walker spent a long time contemplating the cost Hurston had paid for speaking her mind. "Would I also be attacked if I wrote and spoke my mind?" she wondered. "And if I dared open my mouth to speak, must I always be 'correct'? And by whose standards?" [*Our Mothers' Gardens*, p. 87] She concluded that she would repudiate "the kind of criticism that intimidates rather than instructs the young." [*Our Mothers' Gardens*, p. 87]

It was a timely decision, for in 1970 *The Third Life of Grange Copeland* was published, and while reviewers praised the realism of the novel, some criticized Walker for depicting such violent black men, especially the character of Brownfield Granger, Grange Copeland's son. In an interview with Claudia Tate, Walker defended herself: "I know many Brownfields, and it's a shame that I know so many. I will not ignore people like Brownfield. I want you to know I know they exist. I want to tell you about them, and there is no way you are going to avoid them." ["Alice Walker," www.gale.com/freresrc/blkhstry/walkera.htm, accessed 10/17/00]

Walker communicated not only through her writing but also through her teaching. In 1970 and 1971, she served as writer in residence at Tougaloo College, outside Jackson, Mississippi, and she was a fellow of the Radcliffe Institute from 1971 until 1973.

Having a young child exposed Walker to new ideas. From the day of Rebecca's birth, Walker had dreaded the inevitable moment when her daughter would notice that her mother's eyes were different from other people's eyes. At two, Rebecca was an enthusiast of the television program "Big Blue Marble," which began with a picture of the blue-and-white world as seen from space. One day, when Walker was settling Rebecca into her crib for a nap, the child suddenly focused on her mother's right eye. Walker cringed inwardly, knowing that the moment had come. Years later she described the event in an essay:

> [Rebecca] studies my face intently as we stand, her inside and me outside the crib. She even holds my face maternally between her dimpled little hands. Then, looking every bit as serious and lawyerlike as her father, she says, as if it may just possibly have slipped my attention: "Mommy, there's a *world* in your eye." (As in, "Don't be alarmed, or do anything crazy.") And then, gently, but with great interest: "Mommy, where did you get that world in your eye?" [*Our Mothers' Gardens*, pp. 392–93]

Her daughter's statement brought great healing to Walker, who wrote, "I saw that it was possible to love [my disfigured eye]: that in fact, for all it had taught me of shame and anger and inner vision, I *did* love it." [*Our Mothers' Gardens*, p. 393]

With renewed confidence, Alice Walker left Mississippi with Rebecca in 1972 to accept temporary teaching positions at Wellesley College in Wellesley, Massachusetts, and at the University of Massachusetts in Boston. At Wellesley, a prestigious women's liberal-arts school located west of Boston, Walker began one of the first courses in women's studies in the United States. Focusing on women's literature, she included in her curriculum the works of Zora Neale Hurston, Dorothy West, and other African-American women writers.

Walker's writing flourished. In 1973, her second collection of poetry, *Revolutionary Petunias and Other Poems*, was published. The poems in this collection deal with issues of injustice and celebrate the role of black women in the Civil Rights Movement. *Revolutionary Petunias* received the Lillian Smith Book Award from the Southern Regional Council, which honors those who, "through their writing, carry on Smith's legacy of elucidating the condition of racial and social inequity and proposing a vision of justice and human understanding" ["Lillian Smith Book Awards"]. The collection was also nominated for a National Book Award.

That same year saw publication of *In Love and Trouble: Stories of Black Women*, a collection of short stories dealing with the violence in black women's lives and their modes of fighting back—a theme increasingly common in Walker's work. "The cruelty of the black man to his wife and family is one of the greatest [American] tragedies," she said in an interview for *Publishers Weekly* magazine. "It has mutilated the spirit and body of the black family and of most black mothers." [*Contemporary Authors New Revision Series*, Vol. 66, p. 438] The collection won the Richard and Hinda Rosenthal Award from the National Institute of Arts and Letters.

Walker was dealing with her own feelings about her birth family at the time. In 1973, her father, with whom her relationship had grown distant since her departure for college, died, and Walker returned to Georgia for the funeral. Eleven years later, she wrote, "What I regret most about my relationship with my father is that it did not improve until after his death. For a long time I felt so shut off from him that we were unable to talk. I hadn't the experience, as a younger woman, to ask the questions I would ask now." [*Living*, pp. 9–10]

As Walker stood with her seven brothers and sisters at the funeral, she at first felt out of place. Her oldest brother had left home before she was born, so she didn't know him, and her other siblings seemed to have feelings toward their father that were very different from her own. "I watched my sister cry over my father until she blacked out from grief," she later wrote. "I saw my brothers sobbing, reminding each other of what a great father he had been. My oldest brother and I did not share a tear between us. When I left my father's grave he came up and introduced himself. 'You don't ever have to walk alone,' he said, and put his arms around me." [*Our Mothers' Gardens*, p. 330]

Perhaps it was because she was dealing with issues of mortality and broken family relationships—Hurston herself had been ostracized by her family for her unconventional lifestyle—or perhaps it was because she was spending so much time studying Hurston; but whatever the reason might have been, Walker traveled to Florida later in that year to search for Hurston's unmarked grave. She arranged to meet Charlotte Hunt, a woman from Winter Park, Florida, who was writing her graduate dissertation on Hurston and with whom she had been corresponding. After finding each other at the airport in Sanford, Florida, the two women began to explore the area in which Hurston had lived.

To facilitate the search for Hurston's grave, Walker told everyone they met that she was Hurston's niece. After tracking down numerous people from Hurston's life, they finally were told that Hurston was buried in the Garden of the Heavenly Rest, a cemetery no longer in use. Accompanied by a woman, named Rosalee, who worked at the funeral home that had handled Hurston's burial, Walker and Hunt drove to the cemetery. They had been told that Hurston's unmarked grave was somewhere in a circle near the front gate, but they discovered on arriving that the circle was of approximately an acre in size and seemed little more than an overgrown field.

While Hunt searched in one area of the cemetery, Walker and Rosalee waded through the tall grass toward the center of the circle, hoping not to disturb any snakes. Walker later described the scene:

> Finding the grave seems positively hopeless. There is only one thing to do:
>
> "Zora!" I yell, as loud as I can (causing Rosalee to jump). "Are you out here?"
>
> "If she is, I sho hope she don't answer you. If she do, I'm gone."
>
> "Zora!" I call again. "I'm here. Are you?"
>
> "If she is," grumbles Rosalee, "I hope she'll keep it to herself."
>
> "Zora!" Then I start fussing with her. "I hope you don't think I'm going to stand out here all day, with these snakes watching me and these ants having a field day. In fact, I'm going to call you just one or two more times." On a clump of dried grass, near a small bushy tree, my eye falls on one of the largest bugs I have ever seen. It is on its back, and is as large as three of my fingers. I walk toward it, and yell "Zo-ra!" and my foot sinks into a hole. I look down. I am standing in a sunken rectangle that is about six feet long and about three or four feet wide. [*Our Mothers' Gardens*, p. 105]

Later in the same day, Alice ordered a marker to be placed on the long-neglected grave. It reads:

ZORA NEALE HURSTON
"A GENIUS OF THE SOUTH"
NOVELIST FOLKLORIST
ANTHROPOLOGIST
1901   1960
[*Our Mothers' Gardens*, p. 107]

About a year later, Walker took another pilgrimage. This time she traveled with her mother and visited both her old home in Eatonton, Georgia, and the home of Southern writer Flannery O'Connor, which stood outside Milledgeville, a small Georgia town just a few miles down the road from Eatonton.

As a college student, Walker had discovered O'Connor's works and studied them endlessly, but then for several years she refused to look at them because she almost felt ashamed that while she had been reading the novels, short stories, and essays of a white, Catholic writer she had not been exposed to the works of black women writers. But nine years after completing college, Walker thought it might be instructive for her to visit both her own childhood home and O'Connor's home.

Alice and Minnie Walker found their former home deserted. Only two of its four rooms remained standing, and these were filled with hay, but daffodils planted by Minnie Walker had spread across the yard and were in full bloom.

A short while later, they approached O'Connor's large, white house. Although she had died ten years earlier, the house was still maintained by a caretaker. As Walker knocked at the door, she was consumed by unexpected emotions. "What I feel at the moment of knocking is fury that someone is paid to take care of her house, though no one lives in it, and that her house still, in fact stands, while mine—which of course we never owned anyway—is slowly rotting into dust. Her house becomes—in an instant—the symbol of my own disinheritance, and for that instant I hate her guts. All that she has meant to me is diminished, though her diminishment within me is against my will." [*Our Mothers' Gardens*, p. 57]

Walker reflected on the fact that while white Southern writers' homes were maintained after their deaths—in the case of William Faulkner, a black caretaker provided this service—no one in Mississippi could tell where the African-American writer Richard Wright had lived. Painful as that knowledge was, though, it paled against other harms: "What comes close to being unbearable," she wrote, "is that I know how damaging to my own psyche such injustice is. In an unjust society the soul of the sensitive person is in danger of deformity from just such weights as this. For a long time I will feel Faulkner's house, O'Connor's house, crushing me. To fight back will require a certain amount of energy, energy better used doing something else." [*Our Mothers' Gardens*, p. 58]

PAINFUL CHOICES

While progress had been made in the area of civil rights in Mississippi during the years in which Walker and Leventhal had lived there, by 1974 the couple still found themselves living in fear. Walker was isolated during the days, when Leventhal would leave for the office, locking the door behind him to provide her and Rebecca with some protection. The stress wore on both of them, and, since relationships with Leventhal's family had improved, they decided to move back to New York City. Leventhal sold his law practice, and the family headed north.

The home in Brooklyn they decided to buy needed extensive renovation, and Walker came to call the place "the ruin." It took a year to clean the building completely and a total of three years to finish the repairs. Reflecting on the decision 25 years later, Walker wished to Leventhal that they had had people in their lives who would have warned them about the dangers of doing too much:

> Our blood went into that house. And the last shred of the love that had so characterized our life. The plumbing alone cost every cent you received from the sale of your share of your law firm. Every word I wrote was transformed into lighting fixtures, doorknobs and paint. We were not wise enough to know not to try to live in this foolishness. We did not know we should have done something else. At times like this, I felt our isolation most keenly. That we lacked parents or friends who would say: Look how tired you both are. It's obvious. Sell the law firm, yes, but take the money and go to Negril for six months. Write from a resort in the Rocky Mountains, if write you must, and save the money to live on the Upper West Side in New York, in a part of town already renovated. Enough, already! You don't have to keep challenging and "improving" the world by avoiding yourselves! For we did learn to avoid ourselves, avoid each other. Our pitiful attempt to avoid our failure, our pain. [*The Way Forward*, pp. 48–49]

The problems developing in the marriage were not obvious to the outside world. Leventhal worked for the NAACP's Legal Defense Fund, Rebecca built friendships with other children in the neighborhood and enjoyed school, and Walker wrote at home and traveled into Manhattan twice a week to work as an editor for the magazine *Ms.*, a voice for the women's rights movement. In 1974, Walker also saw published her illustrated children's biography *Langston Hughes: An American Poet*. Hughes had died in 1967.

Over the next two years, Walker poured energy into work on her second novel, *Meridian*; on her poetry; and on "the ruin," achieving near-expertise on fireplace tile and floor varnish. But it became increasingly clear that her marriage to Leventhal had ceased to exist, an assessment that was confirmed when she learned of his affair with a white woman. Decades later, when Rebecca asked her parents to sit in on a counseling session with her to discuss what had happened to their marriage, Walker summed up what she had identified as the problem: "I think, I say, that Mississippi, living interracially, attempting to raise a child, attempting to have a normal life, wore us out. I think we were exhausted. In our tiredness we turned away from each other." [*The Way Forward*, p. 29]

In 1976, Walker and Leventhal told six-year-old Rebecca of their decision to divorce. Years later, as an adult, Rebecca described the event in her book *Black, White, and Jewish*: "My parents sit me down and tell me they are not getting along, that me and Mama are going to move to another neighborhood and Daddy will come to pick me up on weekends. They might as well have told me we were moving to live with penguins on the North Pole." ["Mother, Daughter Write of the Black, White and Jewish Family," by Kim Curtis, AP, 5 November 2000]

The transition to single mother challenged Walker, but she also saw professional success. Just as she was ending her marriage, *Meridian* was published. The novel chronicles the story of Meridian, a young black woman who struggles during the Civil Rights Movement to free herself and her people. In the process, she gives away her child because she is terrified that she will not make a good mother, and instead she becomes a symbolic mother of African Americans as a group. The book drew on many of Alice's personal experiences and was praised by critics as one of the best novels to come out of the Civil Rights Movement.

In *Meridian*, Walker departed from the more traditional chronological structure she had used in *Copeland*. She compared the new structure she used to a "crazy quilt":

> You know, there's a lot of difference between a crazy quilt and a patchwork quilt. A patchwork quilt is exactly what the name implies—a quilt made of patches. A crazy quilt, on the other hand, only looks crazy. It is not "patched," it is planned. A patchwork quilt would perhaps be a good metaphor for capitalism; a crazy quilt is perhaps a metaphor for socialism. A crazy quilt story is one that can jump back and forth in time, work on many different levels, and one that can include myth. It is generally much more evocative of metaphor and symbolism than in a novel that is chronological in structure, or one devoted, more or less, to rigorous realism, as in *The Third Life of Grange Copeland*. [*Notable Black American Women*, ed. by Jessie Carney Smith, Gale Research, 1992, p. 1181]

In part because of the critical acclaim showered on *Meridian*, in 1977 Walker received a prestigious Guggenheim Fellowship. The money that accompanied this honor allowed her to leave her position at *Ms.* and devote her attention fully to writing.

Walker also made a two-week trip to Cuba with a group of African-American artists selected by the editors of *Black Scholar*, a journal of black scholarship and research, and the Cuban Institute for Friendship Among Peoples. While visiting a school outside Havana, Walker said that she confronted her own racism when a group of students performed Cuban music:

> When the group of teen-agers finished, we surged forward to thank them. They were happy, open, expectant. Cuban and human from the blackest to the whitest. And then we presented ourselves as "black" Americans (they presented themselves, unself-consciously and without words, as Cubans, of course), and their faces changed. For the first time they seemed aware of color differences *among themselves—and were embarrassed for us.* And I realized that as I had sat listening to them, I had separated them, mentally, into black and white and "mixed," and that I had assumed certain things on the basis of my own perverted categorization. And now I saw that these young Cubans did not see themselves as I saw them at all. They were, like their music, well blended into their culture and did not need to separate on the basis of color, or to present any definition of themselves at all.
> [*Our Mothers' Gardens*, pp. 211–212]

Walker noticed during her tour of Cuba both accomplishments and failings brought about by Fidel Castro and his government, but she was quick to admit that the tour had been much too brief for her to be able to draw definitive conclusions about much of anything. In light of the basic services being provided to people who had spent centuries in poverty and ignorance, she said that "to criticize anything at all seems presumptuous, even absurd." [*Our Mothers' Gardens*, p. 221]

After spending another winter in New York City, Walker decided the city buildings were too tall for her. "I realized I was a country person," she said in an interview for the *New York Times*, "so I moved to San Francisco." ["Alice Walker Recalls the Civil Rights Battle"] She also had an idea for her third novel, but, believing her characters actually appeared to her and spoke with her, she found it impossible to live with them in the chaos of the city:

> New York, whose people I love for their grace under almost continual unpredictable adversity, was a place the people in *The Color Purple* refused even to visit. The moment any of them started to form—on the subway, a dark street, and especially in the shadow of very tall buildings—they would start to complain.

"What is all this tall shit anyway?" they would say. [*Our Mothers' Gardens*, p. 356]

Walker made the move to San Francisco by herself. Rebecca was living with her father that year, and she began a schedule of spending alternate two-year periods with her father on the East Coast and her mother on the West Coast.

Both mother and daughter struggled during this time. "My body was part of a great [story] about changing race relationships in our country," Rebecca explained as an adult in an interview for *The Advocate*. "But with my parents' divorce, that [story] fell apart, and they didn't rewrite the [story] enough to make me continue to make sense." ["Walker, in Her Own Shoes," by Austin Bunn, *The Advocate*, 27 February 2001]

Walker herself dealt with the deaths of first her father and then her marriage by immersing herself in writing. In 1979, her third collection of poetry, *Goodnight, Willie Lee, I'll See You in the Morning*, was published. The title of the collection came from the last words Walker's mother had said to her husband before his death, and many of the poems dealt with the importance of women having a healthy love for themselves. The same year also saw the publication of *I Love Myself When I Am Laughing . . . and Then Again When I Am Looking Mean and Impressive: A Zora Neal Hurston Reader*. This collection, edited by Walker as one more attempt to make the world aware of Hurston's work, was a project close to Walker's heart.

With as much as she had accomplished, the 35-year-old Walker was on the verge of even more. She turned her attention to short stories and began putting to paper the ideas and characters she had been developing for her third novel, *The Color Purple*, a work fueled by the encouragement of a friend she had grown to love.

THE COLOR PURPLE

When she moved to California, Alice Walker found herself living in close proximity to Robert Allen, a man she had known for more than 25 years—ever since they had been students, she at Spelman and he across the street at Morehouse College. In the late 1970s, Allen was senior editor of *Black Scholar*. An activist and sociologist, he had written both *Black Awakening in Capitalist America* and *Reluctant Reformers: The Impact of Racism on Social Reform Movements in the United States*. The two friends had both been involved in the Civil Rights Movement and cared deeply about social justice. They fell in love and bought a home in the coastal town of Mendocino, California, about 150 miles north of San Francisco. Their new home was a place of refuge from their busy lives in San Francisco.

After years of turmoil, Alice was enjoying some peace until word came from Georgia that her mother had experienced a series of small strokes. Minnie Walker appeared not to have suffered any serious complications from her illness, and therefore did not threaten Alice's immersion in her writing.

Walker directed most of her energies toward the completion of a second collection of short stories and her work on *The Color Purple*. The collection, *You Can't Keep a Good Woman Down*, was published in 1981 and examined issues such as abortion, pornography, and rape. Generally, the female characters showed more optimism and commitment to survival than they had in Walker's earlier writings. While critics acknowledged her skill at writing, controversy surrounded her depiction of African-American men, with some reviewers complaining that the stories were too polemical. Writing for *The New York Times*, David Bradley stated, "Many of the stories are flawed by unassimilated rhetoric, simplistic politics and a total lack of plot and characterization." [*Contemporary Literary Criticism*, vol. 103, Gale, p. 366]

As opinions about her work circulated, Walker was absorbed in writing her third novel; but to devote herself completely was impossible until she had resolved incipient financial difficulties. Because the money from her Guggenheim Fellowship was running out and because royalties from the sales of her published works did not quite cover her living expenses, she had accepted many speaking engagements. The fees paid to her met her financial needs, and, as she herself said, "It gives me a charge to see people who appreciate my work." [*Our Mothers' Gardens*, p. 357] But the distractions of travel and speaking had kept her from writing effectively. She'd determined not to accept any more speaking engagements or writing assignments until the novel was finished, telling people she was taking a year off for silence. "Everyone said, Sure, they understood," she recalled. "I was terrified." [*Our Mothers' Gardens*, p. 358]

When she received her first payment for *You Can't Keep a Good Woman Down*, however, she realized she had enough money to live "a frugal, no-frills year." [*Our Mothers' Gardens*, p. 358] While at times it appeared as if she wasn't doing much of anything—taking long walks with Allen, laying down in a meadow, picking apples, or working on a quilt—she later described this period as a time when she was getting to know the characters of *The Color Purple*—Celie, Nettie, Shug, Albert, Sofia, and Harpo:

> We would sit wherever I was sitting, and talk. They were very obliging, engaging, and jolly. They were, of course, at the end of their story but were telling it to me from the beginning. Things that made me sad often made them laugh. Or, we got through that; don't pull such a long face, they'd say. Or, You think [President Ronald] Reagan's bad, you ought've seen some of the rednecks us come up under. The days passed in a blaze of happiness. [*Our Mothers' Gardens*, p. 359]

By the end of the summer of 1981, Walker was making steady progress on her novel when Rebecca arrived to begin the school year—and a two-year stay—with her mother. To accommodate this new situation, Walker simply incorporated Rebecca into the process, listening to what the novel's characters observed about her 11-year-old daughter's courage and strength. The next year, Walker was shocked to discover that a novel she'd thought would take five years to complete had been finished after less than one year of writing.

Primarily a series of letters written by the character Celie, *The Color Purple* is an epistolary novel that takes place in the South between the early 1900s and the mid-1940s. Celie, writing first to God and later to her sister, tells the story of her brutal treatment at the hands of black men, beginning with her stepfather, who repeatedly rapes and beats her and then forces her into a loveless marriage to the widower Albert, who wants only a woman to keep his house and to care for his now motherless children—and whose given name Celie learns only by accident after some years of cohabitation. Albert abuses Celie, and when his son Harpo asks him why, Albert answers simply that it is because she is his wife. Eventually, with the encouragement of Sofia, Albert's daughter-in-law, and Shug Avery, an independent-minded blues singer whom Albert truly loves, Celie leaves Albert and goes to Memphis, where she earns a good living sewing clothing of her own design. By the end of the novel, the main characters have suffered, grown, and achieved reconciliation. In *Purple*, Walker examined the subject of violence between black men and women more thoroughly than she had in any of her previous works.

Walker also explained that Celie's is the voice of her step-grandmother, Rachel. "I tried very hard to record her voice for America," she said in an interview for *People*, "because America doesn't really hear Rachel's voice." [*Notable Black American Women*, ed. Jessie Carney Smith, Gale, 1992, p. 1181]

The critical reaction to the book, when it appeared in 1982, was swift and positive. Mel Watkins, writing in *The New York Times Book Review*, called *The Color Purple* "a striking and consummately well-written novel." He went on to conclude, "Alice Walker's choice and effective handling of the epistolary style has enabled her to tell a poignant tale of women's struggle for equality and independence without either the emotional excess of her previous novel *Meridian* or the polemical excess of her short-story collection *You Can't Keep a Good Woman Down*." ["Some Letters Went to God," by Mel Watkins, *New York Times Book Review*, 25 July 1982] Writing for *Newsweek*, Peter S. Prescott declared the book to be "an American novel of permanent importance." ["Alice Walker," Gale Group Resources, www.gale.com/freresrc/blkhstry/walkera.htm accessed 10/17/00]

The Color Purple was not simply a book read by academics and reviewers, however. It remained on *The New York Times* Bestseller List for more than a year. In part, because of Walker's popularity and the critical acclaim she received, in 1982 she was offered teaching positions at both the University of California at Berkeley and at Brandeis University. She accepted both positions and quickly incorporated her teaching into a full schedule of writing and speaking.

Not everyone was pleased with *The Color Purple*. Once again, readers complained that Walker's black male characters were too harsh and cruel. Walker's response was direct: "I don't like oppression. And if [men are] not oppressing me, if they're not oppressing women and they're not oppressing the earth, I'm prepared to like them." ["Walker's Pulitzer Means People Will Meet Her Characters," by C. W. Miranker, AP, 22 April 1983] Others felt that the book was too sexually explicit or that it presented stereotypical views of African Americans. Some parents led drives to ban the book from school libraries.

Many critics, however, realized that it was simplistic to label the male characters in *The Color Purple*. While Charles Larson of the *Detroit News*, for instance, initially stated in his review of the novel, "I wouldn't go as far as to say that all the male characters are villains, but the truth is fairly close to that," later in the piece he noted that by the end of the novel "several of [Walker's] masculine characters have reformed." [*Contemporary Authors New Revision Series*, vol. 66, p. 438]

The Color Purple, however, was to become much more than a highly regarded novel. On April 13, 1983, Walker learned that her book had earned the American Book Award for fiction, a prestigious prize sponsored by the Association of American Publishers. Now called the National Book Award, the prize is given each year to books of exceptional merit written by Americans, and each book's author receives both a sculpture and a monetary award. In 1983, a panel of authors, critics, librarians, booksellers, and editors chose *The Color Purple*, surprising many observers who expected the prize to be awarded to a better-known book, such as Paul Theroux' *The Mosquito Coast* or Anne Tyler's *Dinner at the Homesick Restaurant*.

A week later, basking in congratulatory phone calls and flowers from friends and business associates, the 39-year-old Walker thought someone was kidding her when a radio reporter called her at her home to ask about her response to being awarded the Pulitzer Prize for fiction. But the question was no joke. On April 18, only five days after the announcement of the American Book Awards, the world learned that Walker had become the first African-American woman to receive the prestigious Pulitzer Prize for fiction, one of a group of annual awards established by 19th-century publisher Joseph Pulitzer and administered by the School of Journalism at Columbia University in New York City.

The win left Walker temporarily at a loss for words; as she admitted to a reporter, "I don't know what I feel yet. I don't know what it means."

["Walker's Pulitzer Means People Will Meet Her Characters"] In the same interview, she described her ideal of her novel's impact: "I hope when you finish *The Color Purple*, you're able to put it down and say, Well, there's a lot of joy to be had." [ibid.]

Ten days later, Walker's words had returned. She traveled from California to join a group of writers, editors, and publishers for the presentation of the American Book Awards, held in the South Reading Room of the main branch of the New York City Public Library. During her acceptance speech, she dedicated the award to her parents, "who have never written or read a novel." ["Award Gala Honors Newcomers," by Hillary Johnson, *The Christian Science Monitor*, 13 May 1983, B3]

The attention paid to *The Color Purple* increased publicity for Walker's first collection of essays, published later in 1983. *In Search of Our Mothers' Gardens: Womanist Prose* contains 35 essays, speeches, reviews, and interviews written between 1966 and 1982. Walker herself coined the term *womanist*, to describe black feminism. Early in 1984, she explained the distinctions she perceived between African-American and white feminists in an interview with David Bradley for *The New York Times*:

> You see, one of the problems with white feminism is that it is not a tradition that teaches white women that they are capable. Whereas my tradition assumes I'm capable. I have a tradition of people not letting me get the skills, but I have cleared fields, I have lifted whatever, I have done it. It ain't not a tradition of wondering whether or not I could do it because I'm a woman....
>
> Part of our tradition as black women is that we are universalists. Black children, yellow children, red children, brown children, that is the black woman's normal, day-to-day relationship. In my family alone, we are about four different colors. When a black woman looks at the world, it is so different ... when I look at the people in Iran they look like kinfolk. When I look at the people in Cuba, they look like my uncles and nieces. ["Novelist Alice Walker Telling the Black Woman's Story," by David Bradley, *The New York Times*, 8 January 1984]

The writings included in *In Search of Our Mothers' Gardens* cover topics as diverse as literary criticism, rural poverty, personal relationships, and racism among feminists. They expand on some of the themes of her novels and poems while also demonstrating her engaging sense of humor.

Walker would soon need that sense of humor as her mother Minnie, who had suffered a series of small strokes during the writing of *The Color Purple*, now suffered from a major stroke that left her largely paralyzed. A period of hopeful improvement came to an end with another series of strokes that left Minnie Walker completely incapacitated. "Eventually," wrote Alice, "all that was left of my mother was her smile, radiating out of a body that already seemed, in her bed, settled into its final resting place. There was not a day, all those years, that I did not feel the emptiness left by my mother's absence, particularly as she gradually lost the ability to talk, beyond a slurred greeting, which, true to her spirit, she slurred cheerfully." [*Same River*, p. 25]

Throughout much of 1983, Alice suffered from fatigue, soreness, and swelling. She ignored these symptoms and continued writing, speaking, and even preparing for a trip to China in June, where she hoped to meet with Chinese women writers. Furthermore, negotiations were underway with Warner Brothers to make a film version of *The Color Purple*, a project in which Walker insisted on playing an active role. While the busy writer and activist did not have time to be sick, her soon to be realized medical problems could not be ignored indefinitely.

LESSONS IN ENDURANCE

As Alice Walker traveled to China, she came to the realization that something had gone terribly wrong in her body. She was having trouble thinking and her face was gray and puffy. On the train from Shanghai to Hong Kong, she suffered a hemorrhage. By the time she returned to her home in California, she could barely put one foot in front of another, and she ached in every muscle and joint. An elaborately carved cane she had purchased in China became a necessity; without it, she could not walk. She sought the aid of numerous doctors, but none of them could determine what ailed her.

At about the same time, Robert Allen told her that he had had an affair with a former girlfriend a year or so earlier. Writing about this situation later, Walker acknowledged that her relationship with Allen always had been complicated by her "creative and/or depression-driven moodiness" and her "deep love of and reverence for women," as well as by Allen's addictions to alcohol and to other substances (addictions which she credits him with eventually overcoming). [*Same River*, p. 27] She wondered, however, whether her illness might be connected in some way to Allen's infidelity, whether she had contracted some debilitating disease because of it. In spite of her doubts, she stayed in the relationship. She loved him deeply and trusted him to follow through on the changes he had committed to making. "I also stayed," she later admitted, "because I was too weakened and confused by my illness, and by my mother's illness, to make such a painful break. The humiliation of being in this position with a black man, at a time when I was being publicly and venomously accused of 'attacking' black men, was especially enervating." [*Same River*, p. 28]

Many of the charges that Walker attacked black men appeared in articles about her writing in general and about *The Color Purple* in particular. Some writers, deriding her portrayal of African-American men, made it a point of pride not to have read *The Color Purple*. One article she found especially disturbing was *The New York Times Magazine* cover story of January 8, 1994, written by David Bradley. "I still feel betrayed by [it]," she wrote in her journal more than two weeks later. [*Same River*, p. 165] She noted that she was particularly hurt by Bradley's linking her "distorted" vision of men with the blinding of her eye by her brother. Bradley wrote, ". . . there is a world in Alice Walker's eye. It is etched there by pain and sacrifice, and it is probably too much to expect that anything so violently created would be free of some distortion. But it is nevertheless a real world, full of imaginary people capable of teaching real lessons, of imparting real wisdom capable of teaching real lessons." ["Novelist Alice Walker Telling the Black Woman's Story"] "I thought I was over any real pain regarding my eye, but apparently not," she admitted. [*Same River*, p. 165] She was distressed also that so few critics noted the suffering of the women and children portrayed in her work.

In spite of her personal struggles, Walker continued to work. Plans for creating a film version of *The Color Purple* moved quickly. The contract specified that at least one half of the people working on the film off-screen would be "women or blacks or Third World people." [*Same River*, p. 176] It also specified financial terms that were in keeping with advice she had received from friends familiar with the industry. Unlike most writers whose books were adapted cinematically, Alice Walker would be intimately involved in *her* film's development.

In February of 1984, Walker met with co-producers Quincy Jones and Steven Spielberg; Jones would also write music for the film, and Spielberg would direct. The three agreed that Walker would write a draft of the screenplay, an assignment she accepted with no small trepidation: That night, she wrote in her journal, "I feel some panic. I want so much for this to be good. Something to lift spirits and encourage people." [*Same River*, p. 18]

Settling into the countryside of Mendocino County, Walker began her work. During the first two weeks, the writing went well, but then the task became difficult. She was unsure of how to condense the necessary events into the number of pages allotted to her, and she felt extremely tired. Eventually, though, the words once again began to flow, and she became confident that she could finish the work on schedule.

"Reading through my journal from that time," she wrote ten years later, "I am amazed at how upbeat I sound, with remarkably little mention of my fear. I just omitted any mention of health. Occasionally I admitted to being *tired*. . . . Not knowing what is wrong with you is silencing, even to yourself." [*Same River*, p. 28]

As usual, Walker was doing much more than writing. She learned that *The Color Purple* had earned the Townsend Prize, a biennial award given for a work of fiction by a Georgia writer and named for Jim Townsend, a mentor to many Georgia writers. Walker also saw the publication of another collection of her poetry, *Horses Make a Landscape Look More Beautiful.* She and Allen decided to open a small book-publishing firm called Wild Trees Press, and in May they traveled to London, where Walker gave readings and both tried to sell the first Wild Trees Press book to English publishers who would release a British edition of the title.

By June of 1984, Walker had completed a draft of the screenplay for *The Color Purple*, as well as descriptions for Spielberg of clothing and rooms, but she would not devote any time to the screenplay's revision. She explained the decision in an interview with *Ms.*:

> I had told Robert and Rebecca that after the novel and the Pulitzer, I would be theirs, because I had put them through a lot; they were always being interrupted, intruded upon. And then there I was going up to the country again to work on the screenplay. . . . Rebecca started having a lot of physical ailments that I understood to be signals that she really needed attention, really wanted me home even though she was her usual supportive and plucky self, trying to give me the space I needed. But I could tell. . . .
>
> And I gave [the screenplay] up. [*Same River*, pp. 176–77]

In the summer of 1985, though, as shooting of *The Color Purple* began, Walker once again became intimately involved. The final screenplay, which Walker had approved, had been written, and Walker was on the set almost every day, suggesting last-minute adjustments. She gave countless speech classes to actors trying to learn the subtleties of their characters' dialects and was constantly ready to answer questions about the details, such as the types of flowers and vegetables that would have grown in Celie's garden.

Few people imagined the toll that Walker's devotion to the movie was taking on her. "I sat under a tree and offered speech lessons and tarot readings, painfully conscious of my fuzzy thinking and blotchy skin, my soul-deep exhaustion and an almost ever-present nausea," she later wrote. "I was unequal to the task of pointing out to Steven every 'error' I saw about to be made, as my critics later assumed I should have, or even of praising the exquisite things he constantly thought up, which moved me to tears each evening as we watched 'dailies.' This pained me; I felt it an unexplainable and quite personal failing." [*Same River*, p. 30]

Her fragile condition did not escape notice. Speaking to Elena Featherston, who was making a documentary about Walker at the time,

Steven Spielberg commented on Walker's presence: "Alice is like a ghost. She is otherworldly. And I mean that in the most positive way. She is here, she is real, but she has one foot in the other world." [*Same River*, p. 190] When Walker heard of his comments, she thought that he was perhaps sensing how precarious her physical condition remained.

Throughout the summer of 1985, as the shooting progressed, Walker suffered from recurrent anxiety dreams, which she attributed to her nervousness about the film. One night, she dreamed that a scene set in a "juke joint" would be shot in a McDonald's and she felt great relief when she saw the actual set—a convincing juke joint. Another night, she dreamed of the noise and gaseous crowd-dispersal bombs of a riot.

At this same time, the making of *The Color Purple* was polarizing the opinion of its potential audience; for although Spielberg followed his usual practice of keeping from the press what he could about the film's shooting, lack of information on the project's development did not stop opinion shapers from voicing their criticisms. Many complained that Spielberg, who at the time was best known for *Jaws, Close Encounters of the Third Kind, Raiders of the Lost Ark*, and *E.T.: The Extra-Terrestrial*, had been chosen to direct. They wondered whether a white Jewish man whose reputation was built on action-adventure and science-fiction movies could effectively portray the story of an impoverished African-American woman. They also could not understand why African-American Quincy Jones had chosen Spielberg in the first place. Jones remained unperturbed by the criticism. "I knew I would take heat for it," he said in an interview for *Ms*. "But there was never another director for this film. Steven has everything—the science and the soul to make this movie great." [*Same River*, p. 189]

Attention given to the movie also reawakened discontent with Walker's portrayal of black men. Some critics claimed that such abuse of black women by black men had never happened, and others maintained that it had happened only in the past. Others acknowledged that the problem of domestic violence existed in some African-American homes but argued that the issue should not be dealt with publicly in order to avoid the encouragement of negative racial stereotypes. Leaders in the lesbian community protested on learning that the physical relationship between Celie and Shug would be only hinted at, by a single kiss, and not developed.

The controversy reached its height when *The Color Purple* opened, on December 18, 1985. Opinions varied widely. Some reviewers honored the film with positions on their top-ten lists for the year, and others condemned it in the most severe terms.

Walker herself initially had mixed feelings about the film. At a private screening earlier in the month, she had seen problems with the characters, editing, costumes, and speech patterns and finally wondered how a project for which so many had worked so earnestly could end so poorly. She stayed awake at night, terrified that she would have to admit publicly that the film was bad, and made every excuse to avoid interviews. At the premiere, however, she was more able to see the film's strengths. "I *loved* the film . . . ," she wrote in her journal a month later. "I was finally able to see *it*, and to let go of the scenes that were *not* there. It is far more conventional than the novel, . . . but I still felt a lot of the soul of the people—and that was lovely." [*Same River*, p. 163] She also felt that seeing the film in a theater full of people enhanced the experience.

A screening even *more* important to Walker, however, took place on January 18, 1986, when she and her mother attended a special opening of *The Color Purple*, at the Pex Theater in Eatonville, Georgia. Tickets for the event sold out on the first morning of their availability, and merchants draped downtown store windows with purple crepe paper. The Walker family arrived in limousines and made their way along a red carpet to the theater's entrance. Walker's mother, whose body had been crippled by her many strokes, used a wheelchair to get into the theater, where she was then seated in the main auditorium in a large armchair that had been brought from her home. Eatonton had changed since Alice Walker's childhood days—when she and her mother, and all other African Americans, had had to use a separate entrance that led to the theater's balcony.

Before the screening began, Walker addressed the crowd:

> When you love people, you can trust them with the truth as you see it. You can tell the truth, and it shows that you love people, not that you hate them.
>
> There are a lot of elders here tonight. I want to thank you for all the Sundays in church—the smiles you didn't have to smile. I want to thank you for the quarters you gave me. You didn't have to do it.
>
> I'm proud of the elders, and I'm proud of the ancestors. I think of this movie as a gift to you. ["Color This Georgia Home Town Purple," by Ellen Steese, *The Christian Science Monitor*, 24 March 1986]

As the theater darkened and the screening began, Walker quietly left her seat to hold her mother's hand. She said in subsequent interviews that Minnie Walker had been the inspiration for the character of Celie's devoted sister, Nettie.

In the following two months, Walker found herself caught up in both the publicity and in the controversy surrounding the Academy Awards. When the awards had been announced, and she had privately given thanks that *The Color Purple* had not won in a single category, she was ready to move on to her next project. While researching *The Color Purple*, Walker had discovered an African custom that offended her sense of justice, and she determined to use this new cause as the centerpiece of a novel.

Taking On the World

The custom that had so appalled Alice Walker was the ancient practice of some African communities of circumcising girls, in part, to ensure their entry into marriage as virgins. She first read of this in Joy Adamson's *The Peoples of Kenya*, which an African man had given to her on the set of *The Color Purple*. She had found in the book a description of the traditional practice of clitoridectomy, in which a yoiung girl's clitoris is excised, often without the benefit of anesthesia, surgical instruments, or antiseptic agents and usually while other members of her tribe hold her down. In some traditions, Walker learned, the vaginal opening is then sewn up tightly, making both intercourse and childbirth extremely painful. In the description Walker read, a 12-year-old girl's genitals were rubbed with dried chicken dung, perhaps used as an antiseptic.

Outraged by the description of what she came to refer to as "sexual torture" and "female genital mutilation", Walker was even more appalled to discover that the practice was ongoing in parts of Africa, the Middle East, and the Far East and in some Western nations. Her research led her to conclude that more than 100 million living women and girls had experienced clitoridectomy. Unsure of how best to approach this subject in her writing, she continued her research while completing other projects.

One of these projects was her fourth novel, *The Temple of My Familiar*. Walker envisioned writing what she termed "a romance of the last 500,000 years" that would incorporate the stories of three pairs of lovers, along with their memories from past lives; one of the couples would include the granddaughter of Celie from *The Color Purple*. The novel was to rewrite history, exposing its racism, sexism, oppression, and violence. As its title indicated, it would create a temple: through words, it would build a structure of beliefs. The book, Walker explained, would be "less about the relationships of human beings to each other than about the relationship of humans (women, in particular) to animals, who, in the outer world, symbolize woman's inner spirit." [*Anything We Love Can Be Saved: A Writers Activism*, p. 118]

As often happened when she was writing, Walker believed the characters of her book visited her and spoke to her, telling her their stories. Some of the characters in *The Temple of My Familiar* spoke fluent Spanish, though, and the expectation Walker reported that she understand them became a source of frustration—the more so in the fall of 1986, when she sought private instruction in Spanish but made little progress.

The word "familiar" in the title of the novel refers to animal spirits, and as she worked on the book Walker noticed more animals around her. Having rejected the Christianity in which she had been raised, she had embraced a spirituality that saw the earth as deity and incorporated many New Age philosophies, and she interpreted the presence of these animals from that perspective. "It seemed to me," she later explained, "that the animals I now saw wherever I looked—much like the Spanish-speaking characters who showed up talking at the moment I started to learn Spanish—had decided to wait until it was clear whether I had eyes to see, and then had decided to let themselves be seen." [*Anything We Love*, p. 119]

At about this time, Walker's faith in the benevolence of the earth was shaken. She learned that the serious illness from which she was slowly recovering had been caused by tick bites from years earlier. "It is my habit as a born-again pagan," she explained, "to lie on the earth in worship:

> In this, I imagine I am like my pagan African and Native-American ancestors, who were sustained by their conscious inseparability from Nature prior to being forced by missionaries to focus all their attention on a God "up there" in "heaven." Unknown to me, however, sometime during the late seventies and early eighties, the earth tired of people, worshipers or not, taking her for granted. I was bitten by three of the ticks that cause Lyme disease. [*Same River*, p. 25]

While Walker slowly recovered, her mother's decline continued, and Alice made several trips to Georgia to visit the bedridden woman, trips she could afford thanks to earnings from her novel *The Color Purple*. She also used her increased income to provide for her mother's care, to buy a home in San Francisco, and to close the mortgage on her property in Mendocino County.

As the controversy over the two versions of *The Color Purple* abated, Walker continued her involvement in political and social issues. When, in February of 1987, Allen and Rebecca took her to Bali to celebrate Alice's 43rd birthday, Walker learned of the civil unrest 22 years earlier that had left 100,000 Balinese dead. Allen commented on how few middle-aged people they saw, and Walker realized that had those killed in the 1960s lived they would have been of middle age by the time of the visit to Bali.

Events closer to home drew not only her interest, but also her action. In June of 1987, Walker joined several hundred demonstrators who were protesting the alleged role of Concord Naval Weapons Station in Concord, California in shipping arms to Central America; she was among 239 people arrested at the base.

That year Walker also saw the final steps taken toward fulfilling a long-held dream. Since her college days, she had wanted to see her short story "To

Hell with Dying" published as a children's book. The story, about a young girl's friendship with and love for an aged, guitar-playing neighbor in rural Georgia, had appeared in an anthology, but Alice had never found an illustrator who she thought could depict the story effectively for children. Her publisher, Harcourt Brace Jovanovich, succeeded in connecting her with illustrator Catherine Deeter, and Alice was enamored of Catherine's work.

The book was released in 1988, just as Walker and Allen were about to see their own publishing enterprise, Wild Trees Press, issue its sixth book, *The Spirit Journey: Paintings and Stories at Bali* by Madi Kertonagro, a folk artist they had met while on the island. Walker and Allen were selective in their choices for publication, and the books usually were printed in very small quantities, rarely exceeding 3000 copies in one printing. Later in that year, they decided that their writing projects left them too little time to continue such a venture; and they stopped publishing books.

Some of Walker's time was devoted to completing her second collection of essays, which appeared later in 1988. She described *Living by the Word: Selected Writings, 1973–1987* as a map of her journey and discoveries as she explored the world and considered "how it must be possible to exist, for the good of all, in what I believe is a new age of heightened global consciousness." [*Living*, p. xx] Reviews of the book were decidedly mixed. While one critic judged that "[m]ost of the time all Walker achieves is banality," another countered that Walker "uses carefully crafted images that provide a universality to unique events." [*Contemporary Authors New Revision Series*, vol. 66, p. 439]

Many critics continued to honor Walker's writing. In November of 1988, she traveled to New York City to accept the Langston Hughes Award from the City College of New York, in Harlem. The award, given to writers who shed new light on the experiences of African Americans in the United States, in other years had been presented to fiction writers Ralph Ellison and James Baldwin and to poet Gwendolyn Brooks.

Walker herself was engrossed in completing *The Temple of My Familiar*. She continued to believe her work was being guided by dreams and conversations with the characters, and she saw the approach of animals while she was writing strategic parts of the story as a sign of nature's approval.

In the critical world, however, approval was not universal. When *The Temple of My Familiar* reached bookstores, in the spring of 1989, many reviewers criticized the work savagely. David Gates, writing for *Newsweek*, called the book "fatally ambitious," and David Nicholson of *Washington Post Book World* complained that the book was "not a novel so much as . . . an ill-fitting collection of speeches . . . a manifesto for the Fascism of the New Age." The book did have its defenders, however, such as novelist J.M. Coetzee. Writing in the *New York Times Book Review*, Coetzee encouraged readers to think of the novel as a "fable of recovered origins, as an exploration of the inner lives of contemporary black Americans as these are penetrated by fabulous stories." [*Contemporary Authors*, p. 439]

Critical disparagements did not keep *The Temple of My Familiar* from remaining on the *New York Times* Bestseller List for four months or from seeing publication in other nations. In the spring of 1990, Walker traveled with Allen to Amsterdam to attend book signings and to give readings that her Dutch publisher had arranged. When Walker had completed her engagements, she and Allen flew to Switzerland, hoping to be able to see psychologist Carl Jung's summer retreat, his "tower" at Bollingen on the upper lake of Zürich. To their amazement, not only were they able to locate the home, but they were permitted to tour the grounds, even though the estate was privately owned. Jung's was to become a major influence on Walker's writing—she would thank him, in the acknowledgements of *Possessing the Secret of Joy*, "for becoming so real in [her] own self-therapy (by reading) that [she] could imagine him as alive"—and near the end of the tour they saw (and Walker touched affectionately) Jung's hand-carved alchemical stone, said to represent transformation and transcendence.

That night, Walker felt fulfilled. "I knew this was the last journey I had to make before beginning to write *Possessing the Secret of Joy*, a story whose subject frankly frightened me . . . a story in which I would call on Jung's spirit to help me confront one of the most physically and psychologically destructive practices of our time (and of thousands of years before our time)." [*Anything We Love*, p. 126] After the visit to Bollingen, Walker knew she was ready to write a novel centered on the practice of female circumcision.

Walker wrote much of *Joy* while living in Mexico early in 1991. She planned to revive the character of Tashi from *The Color Purple* and *The Temple of My Familiar* and show the trauma Tashi experienced in the years following her forced circumcision. In the process, she intended to confront a practice that, she felt, endangered the health and wholeness of millions of women and girls, a practice that, she felt, increased their risk of infection, disease, or early death.

As the year progressed, Walker's fifth collection of poems, *Her Blue Body Everything We Know: Earthling Poems 1965–1990 Complete*, was released. *Finding the Green Stone*, another children's book illustrated by Catherine Deeter, also appeared, telling the story of a boy's quest for a missing iridescent green stone and of the poor choices he makes along the way.

At about this time, Walker and Allen ended their relationship, which had faced various challenges in the years since the filming of *The Color Purple*. In *The Same River Twice*, Walker summarized her view of the relationship's demise:

> The dramatic way that "success" strikes in America is extremely stressful and destructive of certain areas of a relationship.

Perhaps, this being so, there is no way we could have survived as a couple. On the other hand, I accept that I am of a particular character, prone to distraction and content to think of my body and my sexuality as my own; my autonomous behavior need not invite betrayal, sabotage or attack. At least we were able, after staying together and steadily working our way toward the next honest place for us, to separate with increased humility before the imponderables of coupledom, whatever its status and configuration, and with vastly reduced rancor and pain. We are able still to talk, to joke, to laugh and go on walks together; we are hopeful of honoring both the difficult and the good, and especially that place where they meet. [pp. 37–38]

In spite of her private sorrows, including the continuing decline of her mother, Walker directed her energies toward calling the public's attention to the practice of female circumcision. In 1992, *Possessing the Secret of Joy*, her fifth novel, was released, to almost universal critical praise. It also provoked a storm of controversy, though, as multiculturalists argued that Walker should be more tolerant of customs different from her own.

The debate became more intense in the following year, when Walker joined forces with filmmaker Pratibha Parmar to make the documentary *Warrior Marks: Female Genital Mutilation and the Sexual Blinding of Women*. The two women traveled through Africa, filming the procedure and interviewing women who had been circumcised by force. Walker and Parmar wrote a companion book to the documentary by the same title, chronicling their experiences in Africa.

Furor over the issue grew; a Sudanese surgeon went so far as to claim that Walker was sensationalizing the issue in order to regain fame and attention, calling her a writer "whose star is fading." ["Is It Torture or Tradition?" by David A. Kaplan and Shawn D. Lewis, *Newsweek*, 20 December 1993] Reflecting on such criticism, Walker wrote, "It is harder, in a way, to know that my image, and attacks upon it, have been used to distract attention from a practice in Africa, and other parts of the world, that endangers the health of literally millions of people every day." [*Same River*, p. 39]

But more personal concerns were calling for Walker's attention. In September of 1993, her mother, Minnie Tallulah (Grant) Walker, died of cardiac arrest, at the age of 80, in the Eatonton Health Care Center in Georgia. Factoring in the time difference, Walker realized that her mother had died on Willie Lee Walker's birthday. "Knowing how deeply she loved him and that he loved her as much, for all their struggles and failings, made me feel this was a special message to me about loving and healing, about remembering and honoring the love," Walker wrote. [*Same River*, p. 37] It would be some time, however, before Walker would be able to remember and honor that love in her writing.

A Writer's Duty

Privately mourning the loss of her mother, Alice Walker began 1994 by continuing a tour of several cities in which screenings of the film *Warrior Marks* had been scheduled. She did everything she could to heighten awareness of female circumcision, in the hope that public outrage would lead to the abolition of the practice. She acknowledged, however, that such an accomplishment could be achieved only through the efforts of many generations.

As the tour continued, Walker became embroiled in yet another controversy. In the final months of 1993, Walker had learned that she had been chosen to receive her adopted state's Governor's Award for Literature, designating her a "treasure" of the State of California. Then, in early March of 1994, she learned that two of her works had been removed from California achievement tests: "Roselily," a short story about a Christian woman married to a Muslim man in rural Mississippi, was thought to be offensive to Christians, and the essay "Am I Blue?" was considered potentially offensive to those who ate meat. State education officials said that they had removed "Roselily" because several test questions relating to it had been printed in Riverside and San Diego newspapers.

On March 8, 1994, Walker sent a one-sentence note to California Governor Pete Wilson, declining to accept the Governor's Award. She felt that if her works could so easily be tossed aside by the California Department of Education it was ludicrous to accept an award calling her a "treasure" of the state.

After nationally publicized protests by teachers, students, and groups such as the National Association for the Advancement of Colored People and the American Civil Liberties Union, the California Department of Education returned Walker's story and essay to the pool of works to be used in testing. In return, Walker agreed to accept the award, but only as a tribute to those who had fought for her. She used her acceptance speech at the March 25 ceremony as an opportunity to speak for those without a voice. Declaring that what her critics really found most objectionable in her short story was that the main character is a black unwed mother, Walker protested:

> They did not wish to give this young woman any space at all in society, not even in the imagination of our children. And yet, I ask you, what is the point of the rest of us being treasures to each other if any unwed mother, black or otherwise, is denied? She is

the most isolated, the most vulnerable, the most scared, and, I believe, the most sacred.

And this is what I ask of you: to the long list of California's endangered treasures—you, me, the wild rivers, the black bear, the spotted owl, and the redwood tree—consciously add the unwed mother. [*Anything We Love*, p. 145]

But the incident was not quite over. When Walker received the award statuette, she was shocked at its design: "Imagine my horror," she told the *San Francisco Chronicle*, "when, after years of thinking about the mutilation of women, I was presented with a decapitated, armless, legless woman, on which my name hung from a chain." ["Author Horrified by Award Statuette," AP Worldstream, 17 April 1994]

A spokesman for the California artist who designed the 12-inch statuette said that it was a museum-quality work of art that would increase in value; but Walker felt differently. "Though these mutilated figures are prized by museums and considered 'art' by some, the message they deliver is of dominion, violence, and destruction," she said, adding that she would store the award in a box. [ibid.]

Walker returned to traveling and speaking in support of various causes, but she was also busily writing about some painful personal subjects. In 1996, *The Same River Twice: Honoring the Difficult* was published. It not only presented her previously unpublished and unused screenplay for *The Color Purple* and recounted events surrounding the creation of the film, but it also revealed some of the personal pain Walker had endured during that time. She described her struggles with Lyme disease, her relationship with Allen, and the harsh criticism of her writing and of the film, as well as the agony of watching her mother's body fail under the stress of repeated strokes. "Even after her death it is painful to dwell on her over-a-decade-long immobility," Walker admitted. [*Same River*, p. 31]

The Same River Twice revived rumors about Walker's sexual orientation. "I am bisexual," the writer bluntly told an interviewer for *Essence*. "I just live my life. I don't think I have to phone in and tell everybody." ["Alice's Wonderland," by Evelyn C. White, *Essence*, February 1996] She continued to take steps to protect her privacy. Tired of the tour buses cruising by, she offered her San Francisco home for sale and purchased a more secluded home in Berkeley, California. She added two guest cottages to her property in Mendocino County, a place of escape where she loved both to write and to entertain guests.

In April of 1996, Walker and Pratibha Parmar attended a human rights–awareness workshop in Bolgatanga, Ghana, conducted by men and women committed to abolishing female circumcision. They listened to women talk about wounds to their bodies and souls that had never healed.

The two women also showed their film, *Warrior Marks.* "Response to our film—though sometimes hostile in the West—was, in this setting, among grassroots activists working to abolish the practice of FGM, overwhelmingly affirming," Walker reported. [*Anything We Love*, p. 41]

Walker gathered the experience in Ghana and a number of other insights gained from her activism in a collection of essays, published in 1997. *Anything We Love Can Be Saved: A Writer's Activism* discusses everything from civil rights to motherhood, banned books to dreadlocks, the U.S. embargo against Cuba to literary criticism. It provides insights into her creative processes and explains how she integrates her art with her activism. It closes with the essay "My Mother's Blue Bowl," a tribute to the gifts of love and spirit bestowed on Walker by her mother. That April, she began a promotional tour for the new book and, as she often did during such tours, arranged for many of the proceeds from readings to benefit favored charities. Reviews of the *Anything We Love* were mixed, the main criticism being that her passion for the issues she wrote about, which most reviewers admired, clouded her ability to address facts and points of view that might weaken her arguments.

Walker's next venture in writing was *By the Light of My Father's Smile*, which tells the story of an African-American family living with the Mundo, a fictional tribe native to Mexico. A character in this novel finds that his older daughter and a Mundo boy are lovers, he whips her in the presence of her younger sister. This one event drives the sisters from their father and from each other, and the novel explores the lifelong effects on all three. Speaking to Teresa Weaver, book editor of the *Atlanta Journal-Constitution*, shortly after the novel's release in September of 1998, Walker explained the motivation for the book: "When thinking about how to counterbalance [female circumcision and similar practices], it was very clear that we would have to deeply involve fathers in the affirmation of their daughters' sexuality." ["Alice Walker's New Life Mission: To Simply 'Be,'" Cox News Service, 8 October 1998]

Reviews were almost universally negative. "*By the Light of My Father's Smile* is less of a novel and more of what Walker would call a 'womanist,' a tract devoted to presenting the case against male oppression of women," wrote Sharon Broussard in the *Cleveland Plain Dealer*. ["Male-Bashing Dominates Walker's Latest Effort, 18 October 1998] "Cleverly narrated and sometimes engaging, the story ultimately disappoints," judged Trudy Palmer in the *Christian Science Monitor* ["Walker's Latest Gives More Heat Than Light," 01 October 1998], and Richard Bernstein, writing for *The New York Times*, added, "If she hasn't exhausted the subject [of the struggle of black women against both racism and the violence inherent in patriarchy], she is exhausting her readers with what has by now become a mannered and tendentious litany of New Age cliches." ["New Age Anthropology in Old Mexico," 7 October 1998] In general, reviewers objected to what they judged to be a thin plot, heavy-handed moralizing, cliche-ridden writing, and a lack of subtlety.

Despite the harsh reviews, Walker remained in demand as a speaker and an advocate of social change. In an interview for *Redbook*, Kathleen Jacobs asked Walker how she remained such a daring writer. "I don't know how to answer that except to say that I am faithful to my own spirit," replied Walker, "and that is my only motivation. And the spirit keeps changing. It never settles. It keeps moving." ["How She Followed Her Heart," by Kathleen Jacobs, *Redbook*, November 1998]

Nor had interest in Walker's writing dissipated. PBS aired the six-hour documentary *I'll Make Me a World: A Century of African-American Arts* in February of 1999 as part of its programming for Black History Month. Filmmaker Henry Hampton chose to focus in part on the controversies surrounding Walker's work in the 1980s.

Walker's commitment to taking stands did not waver—even if the issue was so small as the control of a local radio station. In July of 1999, she joined forces with thousands of people from Berkeley, California in protesting management changes in the programming and staffing of Berkeley's radio station KPFA. The resulting publicity led to the ownership's promise to remove itself from management for at least six months.

She also took up causes with national and international significance, such as that of Mumia Abu-Jamal, an African-American journalist who had been charged with killing a Philadelphia police officer. While some felt that Abu-Jamal's death sentence following a controversial trial was just, others— including Walker, former South African president Nelson Mandela, and Amnesty International—came to believe the trial unjust, and Abu-Jamal a political prisoner for his beliefs, and called for a second trial.

As the new millennium began, Walker also felt it appropriate to bring closure to some events from her past. That October, Random House released her book *The Way Forward Is with a Broken Heart*, a collection of essays and short stories based on her marriage to Melvyn Leventhal. In general, critics responded positively to the work. *The New York Times* called it "touching and provocative," and a review in *The Los Angeles Times* noted that "Walker's merging of fact and fiction, of past and present, of sex and violence and turning away and moving forward, [was] capable in many places of breaking your heart." ["*The Way Forward Is with a Broken Heart* [review]," by Linda Barrett Osborne, *New York Times*, 10 December 2000; "Poignant Stories that Weave Fact, Fiction and Sly Humor," by Susan Straight, *Los Angeles Times*, 3 November 2000]

Walker spent October of 2000 on an eleven-city book tour, crisscrossing the nation. At about the same time was released Rebecca

Walker's memoir *Black, White and Jewish*, in which Alice Walker's daughter described her raising as a "Movement Baby" and the insecurities she faced.

The appearance of books by mother and daughter giving two different perspectives on the same events provoked personal questions from the media. Rebecca refused to grant interviews. Alice was unusually reticent about her own opinion: "[Rebecca] has lived her whole life with my writing self. My first novel was finished three days before she was born. I am trying to give her the space and freedom to explore her own talents without my judgment." ["Books by Alice Walker and Daughter, Rebecca, Offer Different Takes on Their Relationship," by Ira Hadnot, *Dallas Morning News*, 7 February 2001]

Literary critics, however, continue to wish that Walker would balance her interest in social justice with equal attention to the fine points of her craft. Walker herself remains firm. "I don't care what they want," she said of the publishing world in an interview with Diane Lederman. "I have a duty to myself, to my people and the Earth itself. That's what I try to follow." ["In Age of Celebrity Writers, Alice Walker Is an Anachronism," Newhouse News Service, 17 April 2000]

And her sense of duty continues to call her to activism. Near the end of *The Way Forward*, Walker summarizes her vision:

> We have reached a place of deepest emptiness and sorrow. We look at the destruction around us and perceive our collective poverty. We see that everything that is truly needed by the world is too large for individuals to give. We find we have only ourselves. Our experience. Our dreams. Our simple art. Our memories of better ways. Our knowledge that the world cannot be healed in the abstract. That healing begins where the wound was made. [pp. 199–200]

Walker has been wounded repeatedly, it seems, and from the earliest days of her childhood. It remains her avowed calling to bring healing to her own wounds and, in the process, to offer healing to others whom their cultures too easily ignore.

Works Cited

"Alice Walker's New Life Mission: To simply 'be.'" Cox News Service, 8 October 1998.

"Author Horrified by Award Statuette." AP Worldstream, 17 April 1994.

Bernstein, Richard. "New Age Anthropology in Old Mexico." *New York Times*, 7 October 1998.

Bradley, David. "Novelist Alice Walker Telling the Black Woman's Story." *New York Times*, 8 January 1984

Broussard, Sharon. "Male-Bashing Dominates Walker's Latest Effort. *Cleveland Plain Dealer*, 18 October 1998.

Bun, Austin. "Walker, in Her Own Shoes." *Advocate*, 27 February 2001.

Curtis, Kim. "Mother, Daughter Write of the Black, White and Jewish Family." AP, Berkeley, Calif., 5 November 2000.

Gillia, Dorothy. "After the 'Purple' Shutout." *Washington Post*, 27 March 1986.

Hadnot, Ira. "Books by Alice Walker and Daughter, Rebecca, Offer Different Takes on Their Relationship." *Dallas Morning News*, 7 February 2001.

"In Age of Celebrity Writers, Alice Walker Is an Anachronism." Newhouse News Service, 17 April 2000.

Jacobs, Kathleen. "How She Followed Her Heart." *Redbook*, November 1998.

Jaynes, Gergory. "Living by the Word." *Life*, May 1989.

Johnson, Hillary. "Award Gala Honors Newcomers." *The Christian Science Monitor*, 13 May 1983.

Jones, Daniel and John D. Jorgenson, ed. *Contemporary Authors*, New Revision Series. Vol. 66. Detroit: Gale Research, 1998.

Kaplan, David A. and Shawn D. Lewis. "Is It Torture or Tradition?" *Newsweek*, 20 December 1993.

Leighty, John M. "Alice Walker's Soul-Saving Story." UPI, 3 June 1988.

Miranker, C. W. "Walker's Pulitzer Means People Will Meet Her Characters." AP, 22 April 1983.

Mitgang, Herbert. "Alice Walker Recalls the Civil Rights Battle." *New York Times*, 16 April 1983.

Osborne, Linda Barrett. "*The Way Forward Is with a Broken Heart.*" *New York Times*, 10 December 2000.

Palmer, Trudy. "Walker's Latest Gives More Heat Than Light." *Christian Science Monitor*, 1 October 1998.

Schmitt, Deborah A., ed. *Contemporary Literary Criticism*, Vol. 103. Detroit: Gale Research, 1998.

Smith, Jessie Carney, ed. *Notable Black American Women*. Detroit: Gale Research, 1992.

"Star-Struck Fans Cheer Celebrities." Associated Press, 24 March 1986, AM cycle.

Steese, Ellen. "Color This Georgia Home Town Purple." *Christian Science Monitor*, 24 March 1986.

Straight, Susan. "Poignant Stories that Weave Fact, Fiction and Sly Humor." *Los Angeles Times*, 3 November 2000.

Walker, Alice. *Anything We Love Can Be Saved: A Writer's Activism*. New York: Random House, 1997; New York: Ballantine, 1998.

———. *In Search of Our Mothers' Gardens: Womanist Prose*. San Diego: Harcourt Brace Jovanovich, 1983; New York: Harvest/HBJ, 1984.

———. *Living by the Word: Selected Writings 1973-1986*. San Diego: Harcourt Brace Jovanovich, 1988; New York: Harvest/HBJ, 1989.

———. "My Father's Country Is the Poor." *New York Times*, 21 March 1977.

———. *The Same River Twice: Honoring the Difficult*. New York: Scribner, 1996.

———. "Staying Home in Mississippi." *New York Times*, 26 August 1973.

———. *The Way Forward Is with a Broken Heart*. New York: Random House, 2000.

Watkins, Mel. "Some Letters Went to God." *New York Times Book Review*, 25 July 1982.

White, Evelyn C. "Alice's Wonderland." *Essence*, February 1996.

———. "Alice Walker on Activism." *Black Collegian*, October 1997.

In Search of Alice Walker: An Overview

Alice Walker's short story "The Revenge of Hannah Kemhuff" (1984) is more than just a tale of voodoo. It is a story about racial suffering, survival, redemption, and revenge through "black witchcraft." [*In Search of Our Mothers' Gardens*, p.10] In it, Hannah Kemhuff goes to the "witch" Tante Rosie to curse the white woman who humiliated her many years before. "The little moppet," as the white woman is called, refuses Hannah Kemhuff and her children government surplus food during the Depression because they seem, although clearly starving, too well dressed in clothing passed down through the family to be in need of food. This incident becomes a turning point for Hannah; her husband deserts her shortly thereafter, and she watches her children weaken and die, one by one, of malnutrition. Hannah's grief seeks justice, and, as she tells Tante Rosie and her assistant, the narrator: "I could die easier if I knew something, after all these years, had been done to the little moppet. God cannot be let to make her happy all these years and me miserable." ["The Revenge of Hannah Kemhuff," in *In Love and Trouble*, p. 67]

"The Revenge of Hannah Kemhuff" microcosmically represents the many elements that motivate Alice Walker's writing. This short story more specifically addresses her appreciation for the female narrative and her desire to write the female voice; Walker's own mother served as a model for Hannah. The writing of "Hannah Kemhuff" exemplifies Walker's search for documentation of an "authentic black"[1] experience and for a matrilineal literary heritage, for in her search for sources of "black witchcraft" Walker resurrected the nearly forgotten work of anthropologist and writer Zora Neale Hurston. Finally, it represents her continued experimentation with form; Hannah tells her story in a vernacular that Walker, like Hurston, presents as uniquely African-American.

"The Revenge of Hannah Kemhuff" can be said to represent what Walker believed about writing itself. In "Saving the Life That Is Your Own," the first essay in her collection of "womanist" prose, *In Search of Our Mothers' Gardens*, Walker muses: "[I]t has been said that someone asked Toni Morrison why she writes the kind of books she writes, and that she replied: Because they are the kind of books I want to read." [7] Walker adds to Morrison's statement: "I write all of the things *I should have been able to read.*" [13] Walker's major themes, beyond those represented in "Hannah Kemhuff," indicate an attempt to make manifest the African-American experiences that she feels have been erased from the American master narrative. The most conspicuous of these themes are the oppression and liberation of the African-American community in general and of the African-American female in particular; the construction of a matrilineal literary tradition; writing as an act of beauty and as an act of resistance; and the necessity of redemption, forgiveness, spirituality, history, memory, activism, and love on both individual and communal levels. Most of them are anchored in turn by the psychological and spiritual growth of a self situated within an oppressive society.

Although her themes may, in general, remain consistent, their specific manifestation evolves. This thematic evolution reveals the profound "tensions" that make her exploration of any given theme most engaging. Henry Louis Gates Jr. points out that "Walker's moral imagination is in fact most fully engaged when exploring cultural dualities and dilemmas, the ineradicable tensions and ambivalences of our own modernity." [*Alice Walker: Critical Perspectives Past and Present*, p. xi] Tension, evolution, and generic variety characterize her most representative themes. Investigating the dialogues that exist among these themes is the project of this essay.

WOMANISM, THE FEMALE SELF, AND
A MATRILINEAL TRADITION

Walker's conception of herself as a "womanist" accounts for her most prevalent theme: the experience of the African-American woman as both an oppressed and a liberated individual. In "From An Interview," an essay transcribed from a famous early interview with John O'Brien, she writes: "I am preoccupied with the spiritual survival, the survival *whole* of my people. But beyond that, I am committed to exploring the oppressions, the insanities, the loyalties, and the triumphs of black women." [*Our Mothers' Gardens*, p. 250] She continues: "for me, black women are the most fascinating creations in the world." [*Our Mothers' Gardens*, p. 251] She defines the term *womanism* in *In Search of Our Mothers' Gardens* as:

> From *womanish*. (Opp. Of "girlish," i.e., frivolous, irresponsible, not serious.) A black feminist or feminist of color. From the black folk expression, of mothers to female children "You acting womanish," i.e., like a woman. Usually referring to outrageous, audacious, courageous or *willful* behavior. . . .
>
> *Also*: A woman who loves other women, sexually and/or nonsexually. Appreciates and prefers women's culture, women's emotional flexibility (values tears as natural counterbalance of laughter), and women's strength. Sometimes loves individual men, sexually and/or nonsexually. Committed to survival and wholeness of entire people, male *and* female. Not a separatist, except periodically, for health. Traditionally universalist . . . [*Our Mothers' Gardens*, p. xi]

Walker defines herself as a womanist, as opposed to a feminist, because she feels that the definition of womanism does not include the separatism that she experienced in the predominately white American feminist movement of the 1960s and 1970s, a separatism that manifested itself as a type of racism, classism, and reverse sexism within the feminist movement itself. In contrast, identifying as a womanist allows Walker to engage with the female experience without leaving the community to which she belongs and to which she writes. Most importantly for Walker, her womanist philosophy is a type of gospel; it provides words, a code, by which to live.

Walker's womanist concerns manifest themselves in her creation of highly complex fictional female characters, in her writing about both herself and her female relatives, and in her diligent search for, and creation of, a matrilineal literary heritage. First, we can see her writerly concern with fictionalized African-American female experiences evolve from her first novel, *The Third Life of Grange Copeland* (1970), to her short stories "Roselily," "The Child Who Favored Daughter," and "Nineteen Fifty-Five," to her novels *The Color Purple* (1982) and *The Temple of My Familiar* (1989).

WALKER'S FICTIONAL WOMEN

As Mary Helen Washington asserts in "An Essay on Alice Walker," Alice Walker's "evolutionary treatment of black women" is characterized by the tension between representing their brutal oppression, at the hands of both the white community as a whole and the African-American community in particular, and representing "the growing developing women whose consciousness allows them to have control over their lives." [*Alice Walker: Critical Perspectives*, p. 39] As a matter of fact, Walker's fictional women seem to experience a chronological evolution, in that the female characters in her early work are more utterly victimized by a type of domestic and racial abuse than those in her later work. For example, Walker writes: "In *The Third Life of Grange Copeland*, ostensibly about a man and his son, it is the women and how they are treated that colors everything" [*Our Mothers' Gardens*, p. 251]. *Copeland*, a story of three generations of African-American tenant farmers in Georgia, relentlessly depicts the brutalization of women. Accordingly, the females become one-dimensional characters, for they represent primarily silenced victims of domestic violence. After beating her mercilessly for years, cheating on her, and then discovering that she has given birth to a child of mixed race sired by his own white overseer, the title character deserts his wife; she, in turn, murders the child and commits suicide out of utter desperation. Brownfield Copeland, having learned from his father his manner of relating to women, terrorizes his own wife, the educated Mem, because "he wanted her to talk, but to talk like what she was, a hopeless nigger woman who got her ass beat every Saturday night. He wanted her to sound like a woman who deserved him." [*The Third Life of Grange Copeland*, p. 81] Eventually, in a drunken rage, Brownfield shoots Mem in the face and kills her, in front of their three female children. The only female character that experiences psychological growth is Ruth, the couple's youngest daughter, who is raised by a redeemed Grange come back to atone for his sins.

Walker's earliest short stories, particularly those assembled in her first collection, *In Love and Trouble*, reenact this litany of female oppression. "Roselily" presents a woman on her wedding day, ready to marry a Muslim man she does not love because he can provide her with respectability and security and care for her and her children. "The Child Who Favored Daughter" tells of a young woman whose breasts are cut off by her father when he learns of her affair with a white man.

Although Walker's earliest work tends to focus on the effects of violence on the mind, body, and spirit of the black woman, in *Meridian* (1976), *You Can't Keep a Good Woman Down* (1981), *The Color Purple* (1982), and *In Search of Our Mothers' Gardens* (1983) she more fully explores the possibility of liberation from victimization. This polarity allows her to fashion female characters that are more complex than those found in *Copeland* or "Roselily." One of Walker's own favorite short stories, "Nineteen Fifty-Five," is the semi-comic account of Gracie Mae Still's motherly twenty-two year relationship with Traynor, generally considered a thinly veiled representation of Elvis Presley. The relationship begins in 1955 when Gracie sells to Traynor the song that will rocket him to fame; it ends in 1977 with his suicide. The juxtaposition of Gracie's relative strength and humor with Traynor's increasing alienation produces a type of heroine new to Walker's work. Gracie distinguishes herself from characters such as Mem by her voice: She speaks in a Hurston-like vernacular, the type of representative and subversive "black speech" Hurston documented in *Mules and Men* and fictionalized in *Their Eyes Were Watching God*. This type of discourse is subversive, in that it is simultaneously humorous and incisive. For instance, when Traynor makes one of his frequent visits to Gracie and her partner, Horace, Gracie narrates:

> Holy Toledo! said Horace. (He's got a real sexy voice like Ray Charles.) Look *at* it. He meant the long line of flashy cars and the white men in white summer suits jumping out on the drivers' sides and standing at attention. With wings they could pass for angels, with hoods they could be the Klan. [*You Can't Keep a Good Woman Down*, p. 11]

This last sentence is a spectacular representation of the tension inherent in a vernacular of Hurston's style: while the form of Gracie's speech locates her as a certain type of individual (a black woman) living within a certain culture (the racist South) and evokes all the stereotypes common to such a characterization, it also destabilizes the symbolism of the Klan through simultaneous recognition and deprecation.

Walker's womanist vision is most fully realized in her Pulitzer Prize– and National Book Award–winning novel *The Color Purple*. *Purple* presents Walker's women at their most psychologically complex and, like much of Walker's other work, is a novel of brutality, redemption, and emergent consciousness. Letters written by the impoverished and barely literate Celie, first to God and then to her sister, Nettie, document her repeated rape by the man she knows as her father; her marriage to the cruel and abusive man Albert, who uses her as a mule and treats her as a dog and whom she can identify, originally, only by a title; the development of her consciousness as a subject, facilitated by her intimate relationship with her husband's jazz-singing mistress; and her ultimate freedom, from Albert, from poverty, and finally from her own subjection and anger. Other elements of the plot are, if not fantastic, unlikely: that Celie's birth father was lynched by jealous whites and her mother driven insane; that the man who has raped her systematically for years and sired two children by her is in fact her stepfather; that Nettie has lived in Africa with the missionaries who adopted those same two children; and that, during and after her emotional and psychological liberation, Celie inherits her real father's substantial property and achieves financial independence through her own profitable business.

Although *The Color Purple* sparked intense controversy because of its ostensible portrayal of black men as abusive, vindictive, and cruel and because of its use of a Hurston-like vernacular, when read within the matrix of Walker's own womanist philosophy it becomes an imaginative representation of her most trenchantly held beliefs.[2] In a 1982 review for *The Nation*, Dinitia Smith wrote that "the lives of these women are so extraordinary in their tragedy, their culture, their humor and their courage that we are immediately gripped by them." [*Alice Walker: Critical Perspectives*, p. 19] Tuzyline Jita Allan likewise writes in "*The Color Purple*: A Study of Walker's Womanist Gospel" that "womanism has brought Alice Walker and her characters safely to the land of psychic freedom after a perilous journey fraught with fear, self-hate, and guilt." [*The Color Purple*, Modern Critical Interpretaions, p. 119] As both Smith and Allan indicate, Walker articulates her womanist beliefs in *The Color Purple* through her construction of a highly complex and interdependent female community. As a matter of fact, Celie's emergent sense of self, one that rejects degradation and abuse, is fostered by her relationships not only with Shug Avery (Albert's mistress), but also with Sofia, the wife of Albert's son Harpo; with Mary Agnes (Squeak), with whom Harpo becomes involved after Sofia's desertion; and, eventually, with Nettie, through the discovery of hidden letters. This community of women helps Celie to realize that she exceeds the being that Albert constructs for her ("Look at you. You black, you pore, you ugly, you a woman. Goddam . . . you nothing at all.") [*The Color Purple*, p.176] She also learns how to be "outrageous, audacious, courageous" and "*willful*" as well as to "[love] other women, sexually and/or nonsexually." Her parting words to Albert as she flees to Memphis with Shug express both her newly constructed independence (manifested as a desire for integration) and her "*willful*" behavior: "You a lowdown dog is what's wrong, I say. It's time to leave you and enter into the Creation. And your dead body just the welcome mat I need" [170]. The emergence of Celie's new subjectivity and positive sense of self are predicated on the strength she gains from acknowledged membership in a female community.

This "womanist" community heals more than Celie, for it ultimately transforms many of the male characters, especially Albert. As previously argued, Walker's womanist imperative is a philosophy that embraces both male and female. According to Walker, womanism should not be understood as a type of man-hating; it is not synonymous with male-bashing but rather with the affirmation of a community. In her 1987 afterword to *The Third Life of Grange Copeland*, she asks, ". . . [H]ow can a family, a community, a race, a nation, a world be healthy and strong if one half dominates the other half through threats, intimidation and actual acts of violence?" [*Grange Copeland*, p. 344] The healing of the community requires the regeneration of the individual, and thus Walker's womanism should above all be viewed as a gospel about the affirmation of selfhood. Accordingly, Ikenna Dieke contends that the importance of the self in Walker's work is not limited to the female experience, or even necessarily to the African-American experience. Dieke asserts that Walker's work is characterized by a belief in the integrity of the self, male or female. This belief becomes the thematic repetition of a regenerated self, a questing self, and a contrary self; in addition, the Walker self is defined simultaneously by pain and by an organic unity with all life, "human, vegetable, animal." [*Critical Essays on Alice Walker*, pp. 3–6]

Thus, it makes sense that Albert, known in earlier letters of *The Color Purple* only as "Mr.____", should be transformed into "Albert" by the novel's end and that the introspection he is forced to practice when all the women in his life leave him, the implied examination of the practices in which he was raised and that he has passed on to his own children, should occasion this transformation. After Shug temporarily leaves Celie for another man, Albert and Celie share a platonic reconciliation that is based on his emotive regeneration. Celie writes to Nettie: "I mean when you talk to him now he really listen, and one time, out of nowhere in the conversation us was having, he said, Celie, I'm satisfied this the first time I ever lived on Earth as a natural man. It feel like a new experience" [221]. Albert's re-generation, as a more complex and caring individual, is indicated not only by this new-found ability to "listen", but also by his renaming; as Albert, he no longer represents a metaphoric replacement for all abusive men as the use of his title alone has suggested; Celie's, and Walker's, calling him by his Christian name marks him as a subject perceiving the world anew.

Celie's and Albert's conversions are not unique to *The Color Purple*. Walker had set the precedent by *Copeland* and has continued the pattern through later novels, such as *The Temple of My Familiar* and *By the Light of My Father's Smile*. Grange Copeland (in *Copeland*), Suwelo (in *Temple*), and Señor Robinson (in *Smile*) all experience a metamorphosis when they learn to acquire attributes Walker might well deem feminine; they learn to listen, to appreciate, to nurture, and to manifest "women's emotional flexibility." One the one hand, Walker's womanist-universalist impulse relies on a type of gender essentialism; on the other hand, this impulse accounts for the importance of individual transformation in both her male and female characters throughout her work. This impulse also takes her beyond the experiences of African Americans and helps to explain her advocacy for African female rights, especially with regard to the issue of clitoridectomy, as dramatized in *Possessing the Secret of Joy* and documented in *Warrior Marks*.

WALKER AND THE AUTOBIOGRAPHIC HYPERBOLE

Walker's womanist concerns with the simultaneous brutality and beauty experienced by African Americans extend beyond her construction of fictional characters. Mary Helen Washington writes that "her sense of personal identification with black women includes a sense of sharing in their peculiar oppression." [*Alice Walker: Critical Perspectives*, p. 37] Thus, Walker uses what Maria Lauret has termed *the autobiographical hyberbole*. Lauret defines this as the way in which certain authors consistently document and fictionalize their own or others' life experiences, using this conceptual and rhetorical technique to connect themselves to the communities from which they come and to the communities to which they write. In Walker's work, then, we learn as much about the author as about her characters.

Essential to an understanding of Walker's use of the authobiographic hyperbole is an understanding of the most rudimentary facts of her life. She was born in Eatonton, Georgia, in 1944, the youngest of the eight children of Willie Lee and Minnie Tallulah (Grant) Walker, both sharecroppers. Walker attended first Spelman College and then Sarah Lawrence College before relocating first to Georgia, and then to Mississippi to join the Civil Rights Movement. While in the South, in addition to writing, she canvassed voters, worked in Mississippi's Head Start program, met and married Jewish civil rights attorney Melvyn Leventhal, and gave birth to her only child, Rebecca. She has since divorced Leventhal and moved twice, first to New York and then to Northern California. She won both the Pulitzer Prize and the National Book Award in 1983 for *The Color Purple* and has taught at various universities, including, among others, Wellesley College and the University of California at Berkeley; for many years she was also an editor for the magazine *Ms.*.

Walker claims that "so many of the stories that I write, that we all write, are my mother's stories" and that "in my immediate family too there was violence. Its roots seemed always to be embedded in my father's need to dominate my mother and their children and in her resistance (and ours), verbal and physical, to any such domination." [*Our Mothers' Gardens*, p. 344] In writing about her mother's life, she does more than repeatedly prove to the American public that the black female narrative merits contemplation. More importantly, she translates her mother's stories into literature as an act of counter-narration: in retelling her mother's narratives, she combats the years of silencing and abuse perpetrated on the collective psyche of her mother and other female relatives in particular and of African-American women and girls in general. The autobiographic hyperbole, then, is characterized by a type of biographical imperative. Walker's re-envisioning of these stories can be seen in "The Revenge of Hannah Kemhuff," in *Copeland*, and in numerous essays. She likewise utilizes narratives inherited from her other female relatives: Celie is based on Walker's grandmother, and Shug Avery is named after a northern aunt. In addition, Mem, who represents Everywoman, is based on a real woman who was shot by her husband in Eatonton when Walker was a child. [*Grange Copeland*, pp. 342–3]

Walker's work often focuses on her own life, too. Her collections of poetry are particularly autobiographical and are "[her] way of celebrating with the world that [she has] not committed suicide the evening before." [*Our Mothers' Gardens*, p. 249] All of the poems in *Once* were written in one week, following her return in 1965 from Africa, pregnant and suicidal, and an ensuing abortion. About the writing of *Once*, she claims: "[T]he anger and humiliation I had suffered were always in conflict with the elation, the exaltation, the *joy* I felt when I could leave each vicious encounter or confrontation whole, and not——like the people before me——spewing obscenities or throwing bricks. [*Our Mothers' Gardens*, p. 248] Many of Walker's essays and short stories are likewise partially autobiographical. The African name of the prodigal daughter who comes back to raid her mother's quilts in "Everyday Use", for instance, is very similar to the African name Walker herself eventually assumed. Overall, the ambivalence Walker claims to feel about her own degradations and elations, as well as about those of her mother and father, are translated into a complex web of fictive and non-fictive stories. Her work seems primarily motivated by her own feelings of loss and triumph.

WALKER AND THE CREATION OF A MATRILINEAL HERITAGE

Given Walker's privileging of the female self as worthy of philosophical and literary investigation, it is no surprise that one of her greatest missions as a writer has been the (re)creation of a female literary heritage. *In Search of Our Mothers' Gardens* documents Walker's excavation of a female familial and literary imagination. In this collection of essays, she articulates the importance of female creativity, literary models, and the connection of the author of the present to the memory and history of a documented, or undocumented, past.

Walker's hunt for a literary heritage is a search for visible black female creativity. She writes: "And yet, it is to my mother—and all our mothers who were not famous—that I went in search of the secret of what has fed that muzzled and often mutilated, but vibrant, creative spirit that the black woman has inherited, and that pops out in wild and unlikely places to this day." [*Our Mothers' Gardens*, p. 238–9] Walker attributes the importance of female creativity to its ability to anchor the artist to a real and mythic past and to "enrich and enlarge one's view of existence." [*Our Mothers' Gardens*, p. 4] As is the case also with most of her other themes, however, her desire for a visible female heritage is fraught with ambiguities.

Indeed, Walker admits the influence of both male and white female authors. She names Jean Toomer, Langston Hughes, W.E.B. du Bois, Ovid, Catullus, E.E. Cummings, Robert Graves, and William Carlos Williams as primary influences in her work and writes: "The white women writers that I admire—Kate Chopin, the Brontës, Simone de Beauvoir, and Doris Lessing—are well aware of their own oppression and search incessantly for a kind of salvation." [*Our Mothers' Gardens*, p. 251] She has often added Flannery O'Connor, Virginia Woolf, and Emily Dickinson to the list. Finally, she praises the African writers Bessie Head, daughter of a white heiress and a black stable worker, and Elechi Amadi for teaching her how to be a "willful" writer.

However, as an undergraduate both at Spelman and at Sarah Lawrence she was discouraged to find that no black female authors were taught in her literature courses. "I wish I had been familiar with the poems of Gwedolyn Brooks when I was in college," she writes. "I stumbled upon them later. If there ever was a *born* poet, it was Brooks." [*Our Mothers' Gardens*, p. 258] When she first started teaching a course on black women writers, at Wellesley and then at the University of Massachusetts, she found she was one of the few who taught these writers comprehensively. In addition to Zora Neale Hurston, Walker further writes, she taught "Nella Larsen, Frances Watkins Harper (poetry and novel), Dorothy West, Ann Petry, Paule Marshall, among others. Also Kate Chopin and Virginia Woolf—not because they were black, obviously, but because they were women and wrote, as the black women did, on the condiditon of humankind from the perspective of women." [*Our Mothers' Gardens*, p. 260]

Walker's experience as an emerging black female author in a time when African-American literature, and especially that of female authors, was marginalized to such an extent as it then was, helps to account for her zealous search for the type of literary history she encountered in the works of Zora Neale Hurston. Her "rediscovery" of Hurston's life and work is by now well known. Henry Louis Gates Jr. asserts that by canonizing Hurston, Walker "contributed enormously to the construction of the idea of a Black woman's 'tradition' out of which she and a host of others could write, could ground and revise their fiction. It would be difficult to overestimate the signal importance of this foundation gesture." [*Alice Walker: Critical Perspectives*, p. x] This "foundational gesture," as Gates attests included not only Walker's teaching of Hurston, but also in her editing and publication of Hurston's work in *I Love Myself When I Am Laughing . . . And Then Again When I Am Looking Mean and Impressive: A Zora Neale Hurston Reader*. Walker's two early essays on Hurston, "Zora Neale Hurston: A Cautionary Tale and a Partisan

View" and "Looking for Zora," lucidly articulate the importance of Hurston to Walker's own construction of a matrilineal canon. In the former Walker writes that "Zora was before her time" and that "Zora *belongs* in the tradition of black women singers, rather than among 'the literati.'" [*Our Mothers' Gardens*, p. 89, 91] She likewise writes that she learned from Hurston how to appreciate her own "blackness," for in Hurston's work she finds a type of "racial health; a sense of black people as complete, complex, *undiminished* human beings, a sense that is lacking in so much black writing and literature." [85] Walker ultimately asserts of Hurston's *Their Eyes Were Watching God*: "*There is no book more important to me than this one.*" [86].

In "Looking for Zora," published both in *Gardens* and as an afterword to *Laughing*, Walker acknowledges her own efforts as central to the creation of a black matrilineal literary heritage. The essay chronicles her return to Eatonville, Florida, Hurston's (predominantly black) birthplace and the starting point for Walker's search for Hurston's unmarked grave, and Walker's erection of the now famous Hurston headstone, which names her as "A Genius of the South." [*Our Mothers' Gardens*, p. 107] Walker's preservation of Hurston as an antidote to certain erasures from the American consciousness represents her womanist activism at its most impressive. Indeed, the emotion of it overwhelms Walker when the headstone is in place; she poignantly writes: "[T]here are times—and finding Zora Hurston's grave stone was one of them—when normal responses of grief, horror, and so on do not make sense because they bear no real relation to the depth of emotion one feels" [115]. Her relationship to Hurston, then, transcends the literary; through it is evinced a philosophy that dictates the importance of duty, to memory, to preservation, and to history. As Walker concludes in her "cautionary tale": "*We are a people. A people do not throw away their geniuses. And if they are thrown away, it is our duty as artists and as witnesses for the future* to collect them again for the sake of our children, and, if necessary, bone by bone." [*Our Mothers' Gardens*, p. 92] Walker collects Hurston "bone by bone"—and book by book—in order both to preserve an important heritage and to ensure the continued importance of her own work. She excavates a black heritage to anchor her own work with and to justify its longevity.

THE CYCLE OF SPIRITUALITY, LOVE, AND ACTIVISM

The audacious behavior that Walker appreciates in Hurston and exhibits in her loving preservation of Hurston's work likewise characterizes three themes central to Walker's own work: spirituality, love, and activism. Just as Walker's investigation of fictional and actual women evolve over the course of her work, her beliefs about spirituality, love, and activism as a kind of literary resistance also change. And, just as the evolution of the male and female characters in her work must be viewed organically, it is essential also to understand her other important themes as interdependent. All these themes inform the manner in which Walker delineates her characters and structures her writing of essay, poetry, and fiction.

Alice Walker's spiritual beliefs are dependent on her womanist philosophy, and vice versa. Her womanist philosophy is a type of spirituality, one that arises from her movement away from the traditional Christianity in which she was raised. Walker now defines her spiritual beliefs vis-a-vis her organic relationship to the earth; she has "reclaimed her pagan self." In "The Only Reason You Want To Go To Heaven Is That You Have Been Driven Out Of Your Mind" she writes: "[I]n day-to-day life, I worship the Earth as a God—representing everything—and Nature as its spirit." [*Anything We Love Can Be Saved: A Writer's Activism*, p. 9] Concurrently, in *The Same River Twice*, her book on the writing of *The Color Purple*, Walker asserts: "[I]t is my habit as a born-again pagan to lie on the earth in worship. In this, I imagine I am like my pagan African and Native American ancestors." [*The Same River Twice: Honoring the Difficult*, p. 25]

However, her current stance has a long history of ambivalences and transformations that can be traced throughout her work. Walker continues in "The Only Reason You Go to Heaven":

> For a long time I was confused. After all, when someone you trust shows you a picture of a blond-blue eyed Jesus Christ and tells you he's the son of God, you get an instant image of his father: an older version of him. When you're taught God loves you, but only if you're good, obedient, trusting, and so forth, and you know you're that way only some of the time, there's a tendency to deny your shadow side. Hence the hypocrisy I noted early on in our church. [9]

Walker's struggle with her parents' Methodism is apparent in her second novel, *Meridian*; the main character, Meridian, is a freedom fighter who is eventually well cared for by the black community and by the black church. The black church in *Meridian* can be seen as representative of the African-American community at large. It is the church community here that simultaneously cares for and oppresses Meridian. Within this paradigm, then, it makes sense that Meridian's mother chastises her for leaving her child to attend university and to participate in the Civil Rights Movement while at the same time every African-American community she enters during the course of her travels cares for her.

The tensions inherent in Meridian's struggle evolve into a new understanding of spirituality by the time Walker writes *The Color Purple*.

This new understanding is predicated on an alternative conception of God. Walker's philosophy moves toward an understanding of the earth as "the God—representing everything," even if this philosophy has not yet been fully articulated in *The Color Purple*. Shug Avery becomes the medium through which Walker depicts her evolving relationship to spirituality and through which Celie adopts a new relationship to the earth, to nature, and to the self as manifestations of the divine. Celie and Shug's pivotal conversation about what God means fully reveals a redefined spirituality here, one that has moved away from the cycle of support and punishment embodied by the church community in *Meridian*:

> [Shug] say, My first step from the old white man was trees. Then air. Then birds. Then other people. But one day when I was sitting quiet and feeling like a motherless child, which I was, it come to me: that feeling of being part of everything, not separate at all. I knew that if I cut a tree, my arm would bleed . . . I think it pisses God off if you walk by the color purple in a field somewhere and don't notice it. [167]

Although Shug's spirituality still includes a belief in a type of the Judeo-Christian God that is multiply manifested in nature, this movement toward the born-again paganism articulated in Walker's later essays marks an important break from what she has called the "hypocrisy" of the organized religion in which she was raised. By the time she writes *Temple of My Familiar*, her work is exploring questions of death and rebirth and of knowledge gained through reincarnation.

Although Walker's spiritual beliefs evolve over the course of her work, many of her best poems and pieces of fiction are consistently distinguished by a cycle of forgiveness and redemption, both of which seem to have originated in her Methodist upbringing. These themes serve her new spiritual philosophy well. For instance, in the poem "Good Night, Willie Lee, I'll See You in the Morning," Walker witnesses her mother's last words to her father after he has died. Inspired by her mother's goodbye, she writes: "And it was then I knew that the healing / of all our wounds / is forgiveness / that permits a promise / of our return / at the end." [*Good Night Willie Lee, I'll See You in the Morning*, p. 53] This poem represents forgiveness as a form of individual redemption that is likewise a form of spirituality in and of itself. Forgiveness becomes a promise for individual, familial, and communal growth. The spiritual interrelationship between forgiveness and redemption exists in most of Walker's work, from *Meridian* to *The Color Purple*, from *By the Light of My Father's Smile* to her most recent book, *The Way Forward is With a Broken Heart*.

Another manifestation of Walker's interdependent womanist and spiritual philosophies is her concern with both platonic and physical love.

Love figures prominently in her poems and in her fiction, and the by now familiar themes of brutality, forgiveness, loss, and triumph define it. Many of her poems, such as "Did This Happen to Your Mother? Did Your Sister Throw Up a Lot," "Johann," and "Forbidden Things" all evaluate the revolutionary and often brutal struggle demanded by romantic relationships. All of her novels investigate the importance of loss and forgiveness within a love relationship to the growth of the regenerate and questing self. They also articulate the importance of platonic love in the form of male and female friendship, like that shared between Sofia and Celie in *The Color Purple* and between Hal, Miss Lissie, and Suwelo in *The Temple of My Familiar*. Most importantly for Walker (and probably the reason for its preeminence in all of her work), loving, like writing, is an act of resistance. In "While Love Is Unfashionable," from the collection *Revolutionary Petunias*, Walker writes of her marriage to white civil rights attorney Melvyn Leventhal: "While love is unfashionable / let us live / unfashionably . . . While love is dangerous / let us walk bareheaded / beside the Great River. / Let us gather blossoms / under fire." [*Revolutionary Petunias & Other Poems*, p. 68] On an autobiographical level, "While Love Is Unfashionable" addresses the risks of Walker's interracial marriage to a white man in a state (Mississippi) in which mixed marriage was illegal. On a more philosophical level, the poem positions the possibilities of love and passionate attachments as "dangerous," subversive, and even revolutionary.[3]

Walker does not limit her discussion of resistance to her love poems, for she believes writing is her most important act of resistance and also her most important form of activism in general. Her womanist and spiritual concerns would not exist without her belief that her writing is an individual and communal intervention into the racist and sexist fabric she sees in American culture. Her writings imply a formula: activism = writing = resistance = activism.

How, then, does Walker define activism as a type of resistance? In her introduction to *Anything We Love Can Be Saved: A Writer's Activism*, she defines the foundation of her activism as her appreciation for both the earth and other people: "[B]ecause whatever the consequences, people, standing side by side, have expressed who they really are, and that ultimately they believe in the love of the world and each other enough *to be that*—which is the foundation of activism." [*Anything We Love*, p. xx] Although this quote gives a very accessible definition of the motivation of Walker's activism, her activist philosophy is delineated with far greater complexity in the two earlier essays "The Civil Rights Movement: What Good Was It?" and "The Unglamorous but Worthwhile Duties of the Black Revolutionary Artist, or of the Black Writer Who Simply Works and Writes." These two essays position her as a committed proponent of and participant in the Civil Rights Movement of the 1960s. The latter, however, also articulates the importance of writing as a revolutionary tool.

In a short preface to "The Civil Rights Movement: What Good Was It?," Walker writes that this was her first published essay, written in the winter of 1966–67, and that it won the prestigious *Amerian Scholar* essay award. In it, Walker exercises her early rhetorical skills in defense of the Civil Rights Movement as a century-changing event; her defense is occasioned by "white liberals and deserting Civil Rights sponsor[s'] . . . disaffection from the Movement" and their claim that the movement is dead. [*Our Mothers' Gardens*, p. 120] In order to reinforce the importance of a movement that brought conceptual liberty to Walker and her family, she tells another story of her mother, who, after every grueling day of work, watched soap operas starring white actors. Walker notes that once, "in a moment of vicarious pride and despair," her mother asked her "if I didn't think that 'they' were 'jest naturally smarter, prettier, better'" [123]. At this moment Walker realizes that "black was not a color on my mother; it was a shield that made her invisible" [124]. As a desperate reaction to her mother and as a triumphant celebration of Martin Luther King Jr., "the first black face I saw on our new television screen," Walker begins to formulate a rhetorical style that is both incisive and engaging. Her use of the personal narrative draws the reader into her very real desolation she feels on realizing how her mother views blackness; her movement from the personal to strict argument draws the reader in with the lucid assertion that Martin Luther King Jr. "did not say we had to become carbon copies of the white American middle class; but he did say we had the right to become whatever we wanted to become" [125]. It is this "right" to become something other than that dictated to her that has motivated her defense of a movement that she sees as both flawed and ineffective.

Her fervent defense in "The Civil Rights Movement: What Good Was It?" is translated into a more ruminating defense of herself as a type of movement writer in "The Unglamorous But Worthwhile Duties of the Black Revolutionary Artist," written in 1971. Structurally, this essay functions like a literary apologia in the vein of Wordsworth's 1798 "Preface to the Lyrical Ballads"; in other words, just at Wordsworth's preface instructs his readership on how to read his, at the time, revolutionary poetry, Walker's essay defines and instructs what black artists should do as activists. Conceptually, then, this essay begins to articulate Walker's philosophy of writing as a type of resistance. "The Unglamorous But Worthwhile Duties of the Black Revolutionary Artist" originates from her earlier defense of the Civil Rights Movement and represents a more mature but no less polemical discussion of the possibility of power gained through writing.

A single question motivates Walker's writing here: "[W]hat is the role of the black revolutionary artist?" [*Our Mothers' Gardens*, p. 134] Typically, her answer to this question is multifarious and will remain consistent through the rest of her oeuvre. She contends that the responsibility of the "Black Revolutionary Artist" is no less important than that of the freedom fighter, for the artist's duties include "*the least glamorous stuff*" [135]. This "stuff" includes both promoting literacy and, more importantly, fostering a sense of artistic and racial history. Walker asserts that documenting African-Americans' "*precious heritage*" necessarily consists of documenting a history of hatred, bigotry, and intolerance; nevertheless, she also writes that this documentation can become a source of individual and communal power. Thus the artist represents "the voice of the people, but she is also The People" [138].

Walker's location of herself within the Civil Rights Movement as an activist writer and her articulation of this role as centrally important form the philosophical motivation of her activism throughout her work. Despite the end of the historical Civil Rights Movement, Walker believes her decision to write as a form of preservation, as a form of resistance, and as a form of envisioning will enable her to remain the activist she became the first time she saw Martin Luther King Jr. on television. In *Revolutionary Petunias and Other Poems* (1973), she again presents writing as a continuation of heritage and represents preservation as a type of revolution. In "In These Dissenting Times" she writes: "*To acknowledge our ancestors means / we are aware that we did not make / ourselves, that the line stretches / all the way back, perhaps, to God; or / to Gods. We remember them because it / is an easy thing to forget: that we / are not the first to suffer, rebel, / fight, love and die.*" [*Revolutionary Petunias*, p. 1] In this poem, Walker rhetorically situates her written activism within a larger history of black struggle; this preservative gesture both reinforces and justifies her position. The poem also continues the rhetorical apologia she begins to construct in her earlier essays.

In addition to these works, her anthology and writings on Zora Neale Hurston, her writing on Langston Hughes, and her teaching of African-American female literature can all be seen as testimonies to her belief that the black artist is "the voice of the people." However, these essays, poems, and anthologies do not overtly engage Walker's fraught relationship to the Black Power Movement, which she at times viewed as both sexist and separatist. Although she writes frequently about the Civil Rights Movement in both fiction and non-fiction, it is possible only to glean from most of her fictional pieces an idea of her ambivalent struggle to reconcile herself to what the "movement" became after the assassination of Martin Luther King Jr. and Malcolm X.[4]

QUILTING: FORMAL EXPERIMENTATION IN WALKER'S OEUVRE

Walker's experimentation with various forms is significantly more varied than her relatively consistent use of themes. In many ways, her love affair with different literary forms allows her family of themes to grow over the course of her work. The metaphor of a quilt, itself a piece of art made up of formally disparate but conceptually interdependent pieces, can usefully describe the way that content and form converse in Walker's work. The metaphor of the quilt enables us to see a characteristic common to everything she writes: her work, more than anything else, is overtly and persistently intertextual.

Walker's work fits together like a patchwork; each story, poem, novel, and essay is separate from the rest of her work and yet continuous and contingent. This accounts for the sheer volume and the generic variety of her work. Within this framework, we can read her most prominent themes as functioning similarly yet distinctly in each different genre. For instance, her poetry is her most overtly emotive form. Her poems generally function as short spurts of investigation, into love, for instance, or into the sufferings of life, such as rape, abortion, and bigotry. All are anchored by a profound sense of loss. Walker writes of her poetry that "when I am happy (or neither happy nor sad), I write essays, short stories, and novels. Poems—even happy ones— emerge from an accumulation of sadness." [*Our Mothers' Gardens*, p. 250] In her poems, too, her sentence structure is much tighter and her word choice more exacting than in her fiction or essays. Overall, her poems, which she always writes in groups, are like the preliminary drawings, or studies, of a painter, but they are drawings that have an artistic value and integrity in and of themselves. Thadious Davis argues in "Poetry as Preface to Fiction" that "a function of her poetry, then, is a psychological exploration of self, a mediating of the consciousness of one's very existence and an attending to the emotional determinants of that existence, which is subsequently reformulated and inscribed in her fiction." [*Alice Walker: Critical Perspectives*, p. 277–8] In turn, her short stories are the natural extension of her poetic concerns; they are the tortured poetic self translated into the multiple selves created by narrative. As in her poetry, her language here is controlled, but it is no less lyric. Of her short stories, she writes:

> I like those of my short stories that show the plastic, almost painting quality of words. In "Roselily" and "The Child Who Favors Daughter" the prose is poetry, or, prose and poetry run together to add a new dimension to the language. But the most that I would say about where I am trying to go is this: I am trying to arrive at that place where black music already is; to arrive at that unself-conscious sense of collective oneness; that naturalness, that (even when anguished) grace. [*Our Mothers' Gardens*, p. 264]

In order to "arrive at that place where black music already is," she hones her philosophical concerns in many of her essays. If poetry and short stories are the forum in which Walker explores language, then the essay is where she refines and formulates her myriad philosophies. Her essays are frequently complex meditations on the importance of self, of history, and of activism (although not all of the essays reach the level of psychological and philosophical investigation as those collected in *In Search of Our Mothers' Gardens*). In her essays, more than in any other generic form, Walker writes about the importance of writing itself. The essays are where she is most prosaic, most accessible, and, significantly, most "meta". The importance of metacriticism and intertextuality is rendered all too apparent in the dialogues Walker opens with herself and with her audience in many of her most persuasive essays, from "Looking for Zora" to "Saving the Life That Is Your Own" to "Beauty: When the Other Dancer Is the Self." Many of her essays are characterized by didacticism; at their best, they provide her readers with a paradigm in which to read her other forms, and at their worst they dissolve into trite usage of the autobiographic hyperbole. In either case, the essays afford her readers a pattern useful in understanding her thematic content and formal innovation. It is in Walker's novels, though, that everything comes together. At its most successful, such as in *The Color Purple* and in parts of *Meridian*, this coming together is a marriage of her most insightful philosophical discoveries and her most inventive manipulations of poetic language. The form allows her greater license to explore within the span of a single work. At times, it also enables her to write with greater formal and conceptual subtlety than do other forms—in short, to quilt together more comprehensively the various concerns, both linguistic and thematic, that her poetry, short stories, and essays investigate. Walker shows in her novels how each of her generic forms is dependent on all the others. In general, generic experimentation in her oeuvre is organic rather than hermetic; Thadious Davis has called Walker's generic fluidity a "holistic" artistic practice. [*Alice Walker: Critical Perspective*, p. 276]

Aside from the intertextuality of her own forms, Walker likewise plays with numerous inherited forms. Henry Louis Gates Jr. writes that "like Hurston, she incorporates elements of traditional folklore into her fiction, but elements of the Gothic, of the Southern black migration novel, of the romance, and of the nineteenth-century sentimental novel also appear in her fiction." [*Alice Walker: Critical Perspectives*, p. X] Walker's work owes debts, too, to the naturalistic novel, the epistolary novel, the American psychological novel, the Shakespearean comedy, the epic, and mythopoesis. For instance, the almost monotonous cycle of domestic abuse perpetuated in *The Third Life of Grange Copeland* can in many ways be explained by its overtly naturalistic tendencies. The combination of layered and referential stories, as well as the fact of Miss Lissie's multiple past lives, position *The Temple of My Familiar* as a novelized epic, a type of mythopoesis. *The Color*

Purple implies Walker's debt to the psychological novel in the style of Henry James. *Purple* also represents Walker's most successful construction of a hybrid discourse: she achieves a representational level of deep psychological introspection and evolution of a Jamesian nature through her use of the epistolary form, which in and of itself has a long and varied literary history. Maria Lauret writes in *Alice Walker* that "*The Color Purple* on one hand 'signifies on' the early history of the novel, the novel of letters as written by Richardson, but also Fanny Burney and other white women. On the other hand, it also pays homage to Hurston and other writers and singers of the black vernacular." [*Alice Walker*, Modern Novelists, p. 98] Walker experiments in her other forms of writing beyond the novel: many of the poems in *Once* are written as haikus, and many of her short stories are greatly indebted to the Hurston vernacular. In fact, even *Meridian* is an experiment of sorts, written as a collection of short stories.

ALICE WALKER: HER CRITICS AND HER SIGNIFICANCE

This essay has already discussed Alice Walker's work in terms of her philosophies, her time, her personal history, her formal experimentation, and the matrilineal literary heritage that in many ways she helped to create. However, no discussion of Walker would be complete without an evaluation of the dialogue between the writer and her critics. She writes that in general there are several reasons why the "black woman writer is not taken as seriously as the black male writer. One is that she's a woman. Critics seem unusually ill equipped to discuss and analyze the works of black women intelligently. Generally, they do not even make the attempt; they prefer, rather, to talk about the lives of black women writers, not about what they write." [*Our Mothers' Gardens*, p. 260] Whether this be true of Walker's case or not, her assertion does not take into account the vast critical machine, or the diversity of opinion that her work itself produces.

Lauret's chapter "A Writer's Activism: Alice Walker, Her Critics, and 'the' Tradition" provides a thorough analysis of the personal and literary criticism(s) engendered by Walker's work. According to Lauret, Walker critics either canonize her or vilify her. Those who canonize her tend, uncritically, to "'buy the whole Walker package' because they approve of the activist writer." [*Alice Walker: Critical Perspectives*, p. 196] Those who vilify her are equally trenchant in their deprecation of her work; these attacks frequently, and equally uncritically, focus on her political and spiritual philosophies and her personal life instead of investigating the formal elements and conceptual innovations that constitute the literary critic's legitimate domain. The controversy sparked by *The Color Purple* is a case study useful in illustrating her critics' most frequent attacks. Walker recalls the controversial reception of her book in *The Same River Twice*: "[she was] not only challenged publicly, but condemned"—for "it was said that I hated men, black men in particular; that my work was injurious to black male and female relationships; that my ideas of equality and tolerance were harmful, even destructive to the black community." [*Same River*, p. 22] She was berated for what was seen as her negative portrayal of black men as well as for the betrayal some in the African-American community saw in her use of Hurston's vernacular. *The Color Purple* (in conjunction with her other work) earned her a reputation as a black militant, a female chauvinist, a white sympathizer, and a sell-out. David Demby of *The New Yorker* calls the film adaptation itself "a hate letter to black men." ["Purple-People Eater," *New Yorker* 13 Jan (1986): 25]

The effusiveness of Walker's critics, as noted by both Maria Lauret and by Ikenna Dieke, forces a more thoughtful critical engagement in Walker's work. Walker, like any other author, is sometimes successful and sometimes unsuccessful in her attempts to communicate her beliefs. As Lauret insightfully puts it,

> [w]hen Walker is dismissed as an ideologue whose work is a mere vehicle for leftist, racially divisive, feminist or wacky New Age ideas, the significance of that work as art *and* as political/cultural/spiritual intervention is diminished or misrecognised. *But* this does not mean that it does not misfire, at times, on one, the other, or both fronts. Walker's work, like Walker criticism, is uneven. [*Alice Walker: Critical Perspectives*, p. 196]

Perhaps Walker is most "uneven" when her commitment to her politics and personal spirituality outweighs her commitment to the communication of the subtleties of human experience, as is the case in *The Temple of My Familiar* and some of her later essays. However, some of her earlier essays, especially those collected in *In Search of Our Mothers' Gardens*, some of her early short stories, and, of course, *The Color Purple* give us Alice Walker at her most inventive. In them, political philosophy coalesces with a poetic language to create fictional and non-fictional worlds that are always penetrating and at times revolutionary. Aside from her achievements and failures as a writer, though, the importance of Walker's resurrection of the work of Zora Neale Hurston, and her privileging of "the black voice", cannot be overestimated; these acts really have revolutionized the American literary tradition. Whatever one's critical perspective on the success of Walker's work, it can be said unequivocally that her legacy will be the layered voice, both of black women and of the African-American community in general, that she has given to American letters.

NOTES

1. Throughout the essay, I will use the terms *African-American* and *black* interchangeably; Walker refers to herself and her characters as *black*.
2. See the biography of Walker by Bruce & Becky Durost Fish for a more comprehensive discussion of the controversy surrounding *The Color Purple*.
3. For a more comprehensive discussion of the importance of passionate attachments to the African-American community, see Maureen Honey's lucid introduction to *Shadowed Dreams: Women's Poetry of the Harlem Renaissance* (New Brunswick: Rutgers UP, 1989).
4. Although many critics, as well as Walker herself, have written on her engagement with the Civil Rights Movement, very little critical attention has been focused on her relationship with the Black Power Movement. And, although it is beyond the scope of this essay, a worthwhile critical endeavor would be an investigation into how the precepts of the Black Power Movement may oppose Walker's womanist beliefs—as well as what her relative silence about the movement reveals about her philosophical ambivalence.

WORKS CITED

Allan, Tuzyline Jita. "*The Color Purple:* A Study of Walker's Womanist Gospel." In *Alice Walker's The Color Purple*, edited by Harold Bloom, 119-137. Modern Critical Interpretations. Philadelphia: Chelsea House Publishers, 2000.

Davis, Thadious. "Poetry as Preface to Fiction." In *Alice Walker: Critical Perspectives Past and Present*, edited by Henry Louis Gates, Jr. and K. A. Appiah, 275-283. New York: Amistad Press, 1993.

Demby, David. "Purple People-Eater." *New Yorker*, 13 Jan. 1986, 56.

Dieke, Ikenna. "Introduction: Alice Walker, A Woman Walking into Peril." In *Critical Essays on Alice Walker*, edited by Ikenna Dieke, 1-12. Contributions in Afro-American and African Studies, no 189. Westport, Connecticut & London: Greenwood Press, 1999.

Gates, Henry Louis. Jr. Preface to *Alice Walker: Critical Perspectives Past and Present*, edited by Henry Louis Gates, Jr., and K. A. Appiah, IX-XIII. New York: Amistad, 1993.

Lauret, Maria. *Alice Walker*. Modern Novelists, edited by Norman Page. New York: St. Martin's Press, 2000.

Smith, Dinitia. "Celie, You a Tree." In *Alice Walker: Critical Perspectives Past and Present*, edited by Henry Louis Gates, Jr., and K. A. Appiah, 19-21. New York: Amistad, 1993.

Walker, Alice. *Anything We Love Can Be Saved: A Writer's Activism*. New York: Ballantine Books, 1997.

———. *The Color Purple*. London: The Women's Press, Ltd., 1983.

———. *Good Night, Willie Lee, I'll See You in the Morning*. San Diego: Harcourt Brace Jovanovich, Publishers, 1979.

———. *In Love & Trouble: Stories of Black Women*. San Diego: Harcourt Brace Jovanovich, Publishers, 1973.

———. *In Search of Our Mothers' Gardens: Womanist Prose*. San Diego: Harcourt Brace Jovanovich, Publishers, 1983.

———. *Revolutionary Petunias & Other Poems*. San Diego: Harcourt Brace Jovanovich, Publishers, 1973.

———. *The Same River Twice: Honoring the Difficult*. New York: Washington Square Press, 1996.

———. *The Third Life of Grange Copeland*. New York: Pocket Books, 1970.

———. *You Can't Keep A Good Woman Down*. San Diego: Harcourt Brace Jovanovich, 1981.

Washington, Mary Helen. "An Essay on Alice Walker." In *Alice Walker: Critical Perspectives Past and Present*, edited by Henry Louis Gates, Jr. and K. A. Appiah, 37-49. New York: Amistad Press, 1993.

MARIA LAURET

Alice Walker's Life and Work: The Essays

> You ask about 'preoccupations'. I am
> preoccupied with the spiritual survival, the
> survival *whole* of my people. But beyond that,
> I am committed to exploring the oppressions,
> the insanities, the loyalties, and the triumphs
> of black women. . . . For me, black women are
> the most fascinating creations in the world.[1]

Anyone who is interested in Alice Walker's work is likely to turn to her essays
and interviews as a first port of call, since they—*pace* Zora Neale Hurston—
seem to be the ships at a distance which have every reader's wish on board.
Walker's non-fictional prose harbours a treasure trove of source materials,
from the autobiographical to the political and from the literary to the
anecdotal, with everything but the kitchen sink—no, that too—, in between.
The extract above, from an early interview with John O'Brien, is as good a
summary as any that can be given of her writerly concerns in a few lines: here
are the ironic scare-quotes around 'preoccupations', signalling her
commitment to black women rather than a mere personal interest in them,
and here is the 'spiritual survival, the survival *whole* of my people' which is so
often quoted, and so rarely analysed. Spiritual survival equals wholeness, in
this phrase, and it is a hallmark of Walker's work *as* a black woman's writing
that the spiritual dimension is always foregrounded, not so much *against* a

materialist or more obviously recognisable 'political' stance as necessary and integral to it. 'My people', furthermore, are not only black people but anyone who has suffered and survived with this spiritual dimension intact. The interview continues:

> Next to them, I place the old people—male and female—who persist in their beauty in spite of everything. How do they do this, knowing what they do? Having lived what they have lived? It is a mystery, and so it lures me into their lives. My grandfather, at eighty-five, never been out of Georgia, looks at me with the glad eyes of a three year old. The pressures on his life have been unspeakable. How can he look at me in this way?[2]

Childlike glee which has survived in the eyes of an old man, the suffering that has not destroyed beauty: these are key themes in all of Walker's work, and the question of what makes that possible is explored over and over again. Often, as here, it is done with an autobiographical reference, a personal memory which is the starting point for an argument, a poem, a story, or a novel. What might otherwise be abstract notions or wishful thinking are brought into the realm of the possible and the actual when the author puts her own life experiences into the frame and invites the reader to do the same.

Distinctive as this autobiographical voice is in the non-fictional prose, and effective as it is once its didactic ramifications become clear, it is nevertheless not unique to Walker that she draws upon her own experience in the meandering form that her essays often take. The editors of *The Politics of the Essay: Feminist Perspectives* define the essay form, paradoxically, as 'indefinable', an 'anti-genre', because it is by its very nature 'an effort to approximate, to approach (like the original meaning of essay (*essai*) itself): to approach and explore and "attempt"' an act of writing which is neither pure argument nor mere observation, which sits between short story and academic article, and which seeks to persuade but without making it quite explicit what the reader is to be persuaded *of*.[3] They cite as characteristics, besides use of the personal voice, the meandering movement, the pursuit of subversive and speculative thought, and the fact that many essays are either akin to or originate in diary-entries, letters and speeches. All this is true of Walker's essay collections too, as it is of that other well-known and well-read woman essayist, Virginia Woolf, of whom more later.

It is thus not the form or the voice of Walker's non-fictional prose that is particularly unusual, but rather the way in which it relates to her fiction: as explication and sometimes defence, but more often as an early articulation of issues and themes which are subsequently dramatised and concretised in the novels. Unlike Woolf's essays, Walker's are not conceived, nor do they function as, a sphere separate and discursively distinct from the fiction; if anything, fiction and non-fiction are integral to each other and to Walker's stature as a writer whose activism consists primarily *in* the act of writing across different forms. In the chapters which follow I shall draw on the essays from time to time to show how this tight interrelation with the fiction works, but since this is a book about Walker's novels I also want to discuss the fiction in its own right, even—or sometimes especially—if that means keeping the author's perspective out of it. Keeping the author out is not easy, and this first chapter therefore addresses the *problem* as well as the didactic effectiveness of Walker's essayistic autobiographical voice and the experiential authority it invokes. Roland Barthes has warned us, in his path-breaking essay 'The Death of the Author', of the dangers of biographical interpretation which confine the meanings of what are, after all, texts—that is: linguistic artefacts –to an author's life-events. Literary texts for Barthes, as for me, have lives of their own, and should not be so delimited.[4]

Yet in Walker's case it is quite clear that the author is not dead: she makes herself heard as a commentator on her own work in *In Search of Our Mothers' Gardens* and *Living by the Word*, and increasingly loudly and intrusively so in *Anything We Love Can Be Saved* and *The Same River Twice*. As one who seeks to be, in an important sense, her own first critic, Walker is less a practitioner of auto-critique than an interpreter and defender of her creative freedom, especially where she writes about the more controversial later novels. Since this author's voice insists on being heard and cannot, it seems, be stifled, the best I think we can do while trying to maintain a critical distance nevertheless, is to give it due attention by putting it back in its place *as text*, as a self-representational *strategy* rather than self-evident truth. To begin with I want to extract a biographical sketch from the essays and interviews, in Walker's own words, as it were, and this should serve two purposes: one, to convey the salient facts in the development of this particular writing life and two, to show how the author's construction of that life is part of a self-fashioning which serves her literary–political concerns and tries to control the reception of her work. I am, therefore, interested not in the person that is Alice Walker, but in the *writing* person, the artist. Moreover, I am interested in the way this artist fashions a persona in the essays and interviews through the autobiographical voice, and what kind of critical author-ity that persona then produces for a reader or a critic like you, or me.

Autobiography in the Essays and Interviews:
Life/Writing

Born in Eatonton, Georgia in 1944, Alice Walker was the youngest of eight children in a sharecropper's family. Snippets from her early life are scattered throughout interviews and essays, particularly in *In Search of Our Mothers' Gardens*, where she writes of her parents, brothers and sisters and of her glamorous aunts, who came to visit from the North and whom she saw as role models: independent, sexy, sassy women of whom she refused to believe that they earned their living by cleaning other people's (white women's) houses.[5] These aunts, she says, inspired in part her portrayal of Shug in *The Color Purple* and wealthy Northern relatives also make their appearance in *The Third Life of Grange Copeland*, where they lead Brown-field to dream about a better life in the North. Walker's childhood was lived in poverty in the rural South, a poverty which she never fails to mention when she writes about her parents' lives and about dispossessed people all over the world, with whom she feels an automatic empathy. Both poverty and the South have ambivalent meanings for Walker, and she articulates these in 'The Black Writer and the Southern Experience'. On one hand she feels that as a black Southern writer she has inherited a sense of community as part of the culture, even if that solidarity came out of poverty. As long as the consciousness of being poor is recognised for what it is, imposed from outside through 'deliberate humiliation', and does not become internalised as a feeling of worthlessness, then the community of poverty can be a positive thing, enabling an interdependence without shame.[6] On the other hand, Walker also notes that Southern black life is not something to be romanticised, because it was determined by hard work in the fields, poor housing and the greed and ruthlessness of white employers who worked her parents nearly to death. For Southern black writers, this means they have a legacy of love and hate to draw on, but also an 'enormous richness and beauty'.[7]

This is evident in the way that Walker has passed on some of her Southern heritage in her fiction. Childhood memories of happiness come from the stories that her mother told her, the rural environment of Eatonton, and her friendship with the old man Mr Sweet, who inspired the short story 'To Hell with Dying' which was later issued as a book for children. One of her mother's stories about life in the South during the Depression was the source for 'The Revenge of Hannah Kemhuff'; both stories in turn connect with two of Walker's favourite figures of the Harlem Renaissance, Zora Neale Hurston and Langston Hughes, whose biography Walker wrote, also for children.[8] *Langston Hughes: American Poet* (1974), *Finding the Green Stone* (1991) and *To Hell with Dying* (1988), the latter two illustrated by Catherine

Deeter, together constitute Alice Walker's (little known) children's writing, in which she takes on her mother's role as a storyteller and preserver of the cultural heritage of the black South.

Unlike the closeness Walker experienced with her mother, however, the relationship she had with her father and brothers appears to have been much more distant and negative, marked as it was by sexism and violence. It seems that her exposure of domestic abuse in the fiction had its parallels at home. In 'Beauty: When the Other Dancer Is the Self' she divides her memory of childhood in two as a before-and-after experience of violence:

> It was great fun being cute. But then, one day, it ended.
> I am eight years old and a tomboy. [. . . .] Then my parents decide
> to buy my brothers guns [. . . .] Because I am a girl, I do not get
> a gun. Instantly I am relegated to the position of Indian. [. . . .]
> One day . . . holding my bow and arrow and looking out towards
> the fields, I feel an incredible blow in my right eye. I look down
> just in time to see my brother lower his gun.[9]

This event is constructed and reconstructed as a formative experience in various essays and interviews; evidently it changed Walker from being everybody's (and her own) darling into a victim marked by a disfiguring scar. Only when her daughter Rebecca's adoring gaze, years later, identifies the scar tissue as a 'world' in her mother's eye is that disfiguration redefined and the victim transformed into a survivor.[10] Later still, Walker recounts the trauma of being blinded by her brother as her mode identification with women who have undergone genital mutilation in Africa, and this becomes the central theme of *Possessing the Secret of Joy* and *Warrior Marks*. Because of the shooting then her childhood is effectively over at the age of eight, but the death of the child gives birth to the writer: '[F]rom my solitary, lonely position, the position of an outcast. . . I began to really see people and things, to really notice relationships and to learn to be patient enough to see how they turned out. [. . . .] I felt old . . . and read stories and began to write poems.'[11] Walker's adolescence in the essays and interviews is largely passed over in silence, but the implication is that this prematurely 'old' girl now felt more at home and at ease in the life of the mind than she did in her family and in her own body. Nevertheless, that family does try to support her financially when in 1961 Walker goes to Spelman College, Atlanta. She finds the institutional environment stifling (in terms reminiscent of Saxon College in *Meridian*) and two years later she flees to freedom: Sarah Lawrence College in Westchester, New York.[12] The world now begins to open up, literally when she travels to Africa in 1964, and intellectually too. At Sarah Lawrence she is taught by the poet Muriel Rukeyser, who encourages her writing and passes her poems on to Langston Hughes; Hughes will be instrumental in the publication of the first collection of poems, *Once*, in

1968.[13] Before that, another traumatic experience occurs when Walker finds herself involuntarily pregnant whilst at college. She feels suicidal and undergoes an illegal abortion, but this second 'scarring' produces the same creative impulse as the first: 'That week I wrote without stopping . . . almost all of the poems in *Once*.'[14]

By then, the mid-1960s, Walker is already involved in the Civil Rights Movement, another experience which she consistently cites as crucial to her development as a writer. *In Search of Our Mothers' Gardens* contains several essays on Civil Rights, especially on Dr Martin Luther King Jr who first appears in her life on the TV news, interrupting the soap opera Alice and her mother are watching. King and the movement make a big impression:

> Because of the Movement, because of an awakened faith in the newness and imagination of the human spirit, because of 'black and white together'—for the first time in our history in some human relationship on and off tv—because of the beatings, the arrests, the hell of battle during the past years, I have fought harder for my life and for a chance to be myself . . . than I had ever done before. [. . . .] Now there was a chance at that other that Jesus meant when He said we could not live by bread alone.[15]

In this early essay, 'The Civil Rights Movement: What Good Was It?' Walker's allegiance to the movement's Christian, non-violent and redemptive philosophy still shows in that last line. It is an ethos of which she will retain the pacifism and the notion of suffering-as-healing, minus the Christianity which she comes to reject (again, this shift is charted in *Meridian*).

Walker is involved in Civil Rights campaigns from 1965 until 1968. She canvasses for voter-registration in her native Georgia, and is employed by Headstart in Mississippi to teach black history to adults for SNCC, the Student Non-violent Co-ordinating Committee. Teaching, as a form of activism, turns out to be hard work, not least because the white bias of bible stories has been internalised by Southern black people:

> Try to tell a sixty-year old delta woman that black men invented anything, black women wrote sonnets, that black people long ago were every bit the human beings they are today. Try to tell her that kinky hair is delightful. Chances are that she will begin to talk 'Bible' to you, and you will discover to your dismay that the lady still believes in the curse of Ham.[16]

Despite this insight into the pernicious ideological effects of (white) Christianity, 'black and white together' nevertheless remains Walker's creed, and in 1967 she marries the Jewish Civil Rights lawyer Mel Leventhal. Their life together in Jackson, Mississippi at a time when interracial marriage is still illegal, is both strengthened by the comradeship of being involved in the same cause and marred by others' prejudice. In an essay written in 1980 Walker recalls that her literary work in the 1960s 'was often dismissed by black reviewers "because of my life style", a euphemism for my interracial marriage'. Often her critics were themselves interracially married, or they admired the work of writers who were (Wright, Toomer, Hughes, Baldwin, LeRoi Jones) and so, Walker concludes, the 'traitorous union' in itself could not have been the problem, but rather 'that I, a black woman, had dared to exercise the same prerogative as they'.[17] That prerogative, embattled as it was, results in the birth of Rebecca Leventhal Walker in 1969, which was 'miraculous', in Walker's words, both because she helps her father evade the draft and because she arrives three days after the completion of *The Third Life of Grange Copeland* (in which the birth of Ruth—named after Walker's sister—is described as 'miraculous' too).[18] Perhaps because of motherhood, perhaps because of burn-out and the Civil Rights Movement's loss of momentum in the South after Dr King's death, Walker's activism shifts around about this time to the North and to teaching and writing rather than campaigning in the South. As an academic at the upper-class and largely white Wellesley College (for women) in New England she designs a course in black women's writing ('the first one I think, ever'), which includes such authors as Zora Neale Hurston, Nella Larsen, Frances Ellen Watkins Harper, Ann Petry and Paule Marshall.[19] She finds that in such a privileged environment consciousness-raising of students, but primarily of faculty, is badly needed. In *'One* Child of One's Own' Walker writes, famously, of *The Female Imagination*, Patricia Meyer Spacks's book of feminist criticism which doesn't deal with any black women writers at all. Spacks defends this omission by quoting the psychologist Phyllis Chesler, who wrote that she has '"no theory to offer of Third World female psychology in America" [because] "As a white woman, I am reluctant and unable to construct theories about experiences I haven't had."' Spacks agrees with this statement and adds that she is only interested in texts which *"describe familiar experience, belong to a familiar cultural setting"'* [Alice Walker's italics], but recognises that the matter of why she selected only texts from women in 'the Anglo-American tradition' is not thereby fully settled. Walker then answers Spacks's guilt-ridden question:

> Why only these? Because they are white, and middle class, and because, to Spacks, female imagination is only that. Perhaps, however, this *is* the white female imagination, one that is 'reluctant *and unable* to construct theories about experiences I haven't had.' (Yet Spacks never lived in nineteenth-century Yorkshire, so why theorize about the Brontës?)[20]

This passage offers the most succinct demolition of identity politics in the classroom you could wish for, and one which still applies whenever the notion of experience is invoked as an excuse for ignorance—or indeed, guilt. However mixed Walker's feelings about herself as a teacher may have been, it is clear from this and other examples in the first two essay collections (and in the Zora Neale Hurston reader *I Love Myself When I Am Laughing*, which she edited in 1979) that her didactic sense was sharply honed and, when applied in her literary work, proved extremely effective. Frustration may nevertheless have induced Walker to shift her attention from academic teaching to writing. From the mid-1960s on she had been receiving awards and fellowships which periodically enabled her to find the solitude necessary for sustained creative work, and these become more frequent in the 1970s and 1980s, allowing her to devote herself full time to her art. A Radcliffe Institute Fellowship, for example, enables her to write *In Love and Trouble* and *Meridian*; she obtains Guggenheim and National Endowment for the Arts Fellowships in 1979 to work on *The Color Purple*, which wins her both the Pulitzer Prize and the National Book Award in 1983. *The Color Purple* is a turning point in Walker's career in more ways than one. For the writing of it, she moves to California in 1977, taking up dual residence in San Francisco and in the countryside around Mendocino. The latter, she explains in 'Writing *The Color Purple*', was necessary because her characters demanded to get out of the city and into an environment as close to their native Georgia as possible, 'only it was more beautiful and the local swimming hole was not segregated', she adds archly.[21] At this time she also divorces Mel Leventhal and sets up home with the black writer Robert Allen and her daughter Rebecca. Even bigger changes are afoot now. Publication of *The Color Purple* brings popular and establishment acclaim, which launches her into the public eye in a way that she had not been before. It also brings her into contact with Steven Spielberg and Quincy Jones, who want to make a film of *The Color Purple*, and into critical controversy with Oakland schools and—later—black community groups who object to the novel and the film because of their depiction of lesbianism, sexual violence and domestic abuse.[22] Walker gives a measured riposte to such criticism in the essay 'In the Closet of the Soul':

> An early disappointment to me in some black men's response to my work [Meridian and The Third Life of Grange Copeland] is their apparent inability to empathize with black women's suffering under sexism.[. . . .] A book and movie that urged us to look at the oppression of women and children by men (and, to a lesser degree, by women) became the opportunity by which black men drew attention to themselves—not in an effort to rid themselves of the desire or the tendency to oppress women and children, but, instead, to claim that inasmuch as a 'negative' picture of them was presented to the world, they were, in fact, the ones *being* oppressed.[23]

In *The Same River Twice* this defence of *The Color Purple* continues, in great detail and at great length: it is a big book entirely devoted to the making of the film, the critical controversy, correspondence with Spielberg and Jones, letters and articles of support from friends, and so on. It may be that the perceived necessity for such a book testifies to the importance of *The Color Purple* as a catalyst for (African) American cultural debate, but it also seems that from this point on, round about 1983, Walker's non-fictional writing takes on a different hue. The autobiographical voice, by now represented in the essays as that of a self-styled recluse in the northern California foothills, is less didactically instrumental in the making of a larger social or political argument, or illustrative of an experiment in creative thinking (an *essai proprement dit*) than defensive and sometimes merely self-serving. Increasingly the personal accounts of the late 1980s and 1990s concern what can be dismissed as 'lifestyle politics', or more accurately described as the author's awakening to new age thinking. Clearly, in *Living by the Word* and especially *Anything We Love Can Be Saved*, California has left its mark. Among the more serious and enlightening essays are those on Native American culture and history; Walker's identification with the cause of Native Americans is of long standing, as the childhood memory of her binding in which she positioned herself—naively, but in retrospect significantly—as an 'Indian' shows. But children's play is not the only cultural script in which Indians and little girls are destined to lose. Historically, slavery and miscegenation bound African- and Native Americans together:

> We have been slaves *here* and we have been slaves *there*. The white great-grandfathers abused and sold us *here* and our black great-grandfathers abused and sold us *there*. [. . . .] We are the mestizos of North America. We are black, yes, but we are 'white', too, and we are red. To attempt to function as only one, when you are really two or three, leads, I believe, to psychic illness: 'white' people have shown us the madness of that. (Imagine the psychic liberation of white people if they understood that probably no one on the planet is genetically 'white'.)[24]

In this essay, 'In the Closet of the Soul', Walker characteristically brings her Cherokee grandmother into the historical picture as well as her great-great-grandfather, a white slave-owner. Such a view of racial and cultural hybridity links her, again, to Zora Neale Hurston, who had very similar ideas, but it also has earned her the opprobrium of black nationalists for whom this rejection of racial/cultural authenticity is anathema. The poet and writer K. T. H. Cheatwood is cited, in the same essay, as saying that Walker in effect refuses black identity and that, moreover, she has consequently become the darling of the liberal establishment (at the expense of Toni

Morrison, he feels—but this is before *Beloved*), because she purportedly seeks to divide the black community in her criticism of black men.[25] None of this has deflected Walker, however, from the true path of spiritual healing as she sees it, guided by a philosophy combining elements of Native and African American 'folk' belief with ecology, animal rights and, of course, womanism and bisexuality ('homospirituality'). 'Paganism' is what she calls this philosophy, and we find an early articulation of it in an interview:

> If there is one thing African-Americans have retained of their African heritage, it is probably animism: a belief that makes it possible to view all creation as living, as being inhabited by spirit. This belief encourages knowledge perceived intuitively. It does not surprise me, personally, that scientists are now discovering that trees, plants, flowers have feelings . . . emotions, that they shrink when yelled at; that they faint when an evil person is about to hurt them.[26]

This was as early as 1973. In a speech delivered at a Theological Seminary in 1995, the same ideas are advanced as the result of a personal spiritual quest:

> 'Pagan' means 'of the land, country dweller, peasant', all of which my family was. It also means a person whose primary relationship is with Nature and the Earth [cf. Native Americans] . . . [B]ut there was no way to ritually express the magical intimacy we felt with Creation without being accused of, or ridiculed for, indulging in 'heathenism', that other word for paganism.[. . . .] In fact, millions of people were broken, physically and spiritually . . . for nearly two millennia, as the orthodox Christian church 'saved' them from their traditional worship of the Great Mystery they perceived in Nature.[27]

Paganism, which constructs nature as a goddess and the mother of all life, enables Walker not only to connect her family history with African and Native American thinking, it also unites her womanist interest in ancient goddess worship with the theory of creativity, gender and childhood trauma that she finds articulated in the work of Carl Jung and that of Jungian analysts such as Alice Miller.[28] Both *The Temple of My Familiar*, where Miss Lissie is its high priestess, and *Possessing the Secret of Joy* preach this hybrid philosophy on virtually every page, as do the two volumes of non-fictional prose writings Walker has published most recently, *The Same River Twice* and *Anything We Love Can Be Saved*. The latter bring us up to date with her life/writing, documenting as they do her domestic life, the split with Robert Allen, her relationship with her daughter, the death of her mother and brother and the depression she suffered after contracting Lyme's disease whilst writing *The Temple of My Familiar*.

LIFE/WRITING AND THE AUTHOR'S PERSONA: WHAT CAN A CRITIC DO?

While 'paganism' puts a name to Walker's thought and gives it a history (as long as humanity, she would say), as well as respectability in the scholarly references mentioned in her fiction and non-fiction alike, this does not mean that every articulation, explanation or dramatisation of what some see as crackpot ideas (notably in *The Temple of My Familiar*) is equally successful. Although the autobiographical voice was always didactic, in the later non-fictional writings the earnestness of conviction and loss of self-irony in that voice undermine its political edge. They signal, in my view, a lack of connection with a readership that cannot be assumed to confine itself to the Bay area or to comfortable middle-class existence; 'not by bread alone' now seems to mean rejecting not just a vapid consumerism, but materialism (in the political sense) altogether. Discursive and cultural distinctions between the privileged and the dispossessed are no longer made in Walker's ever-widening global consciousness, which subsumes the other into the self. Of her campaigning in Africa against female genital mutilation she writes, for example, that 'Presenting my own suffering and psychic healing has been a powerful encouragement, I've found, to victims of mutilation who are ashamed or reluctant to speak of their struggle. Telling my own story in this context has also strengthened me, an unanticipated gift.'[29] In this context, the autobiographically informed empathy may indeed have been useful, but in *Anything We Love Can Be Saved* 'telling my own story' becomes paramount in essay after letter after autobiographical sketch, whether they be ostensibly about Cuba, Winnie Mandela, the Million Man March or the cat Frida. As often as not the reader is left bewildered by this barrage of self-revelation, however much it may have been intended as 'powerful encouragement'. Take, for example, this passage in 'A Letter to President Clinton':

> America at the moment is like a badly wounded parent, the aging, spent, and scared offspring of all the dysfunctional families of the multitudes of tribes who settled here. It is the medicine of compassionate understanding that must be administered now, immediately, on a daily basis, indiscriminately.[30]

Similar notions or sentiments—for 'sentiment' is what it is here—of the nation as a family and government as a bad parent, are expressed in the later novels where they can work metaphorically because of the visionary qualities of Walker's creative prose. Here, by contrast, they seem simply misplaced and misdirected, especially when Walker ends her letter saying that in spite of her criticism of Clinton's boycott of Cuba, she 'cares about' him, Hillary and their daughter, but also about the Cuban people: 'Whenever you hurt them, or help them, please think of me',—as if that would, or rather *should* make a difference.[31]

The issue is not whether Walker's new age philosophy is valid, useful, interesting or agreeable to her well-nigh global readership or to her critics. I, for one, have no quarrel with paganism *per se*—if anything, it is too all-encompassing, too utopian and right-on culturally diverse to be objectionable, and that is precisely the problem: it would be like objecting to happiness, or sleeping babies. What one *can* be validly critical of, however, is the form it often takes in the later autobiographical writings, as in the instances cited above. Afterwords to *The Color Purple* and *Possessing the Secret of Joy*, essays about *The Temple of My Familiar* in *Anything We Love Can Be Saved*, the book version of *Warrior Marks* and the 'Meditation on Life, Spirit, Art, and the Making of the Film *The Color Purple* Ten Years Later' which is *The Same River Twice* all function as, even if they were not intended to be, authorial interventions in the critical debate that Walker's work has generated. It is as if she is trying to control the reception of her fiction in ways which then will not let that fiction live—as text and as creative work beyond the reach of authorial possession. This, of course, is where literary criticism comes in, for critics are of a far more diverse plumage than single authors can be and therefore bring multiple perspectives to bear on texts without claiming that any one is the final word. Like many creative writers, Walker dislikes criticism because she sees it—not as a forum where meanings are opened up, but as an exercise in closed-mindedness:

> Criticism is something that I don't fully approve of, because I think for the critic it must be very painful to always look at things in a critical way. I think you miss so much. And you have to sort of shape everything you see to the way you're prepared to see it.[32]

This is a bit much coming from the cultural critic which Alice Walker also is; it is as if that aspect of her creative work is here disavowed. Recently, in 'Getting as Black as My Daddy: Thoughts on the Unhelpful Aspects of Destructive Criticism' she has written about criticism when it is abusive and anonymous and comes in the morning post, as 'verbal battering'. When it is simply critical of her autobiographical writing and printed in *The Village Voice*, she represents it as a form of censorship or self-censorship, something which stifles her creativity. The form of 'Getting as Black as My Daddy' enacts this self-censorship; the essay is unfinished 'as a demonstration of what, because of battering rather than constructive criticism, is sometimes lost'.[33] What gets lost as well in this rhetorical ploy, however, is again a sense of perspective and discursive difference: a critical review is not hate mail, just as 'constructive criticism' cannot be equated with fan mail either. Alice Walker's life/writing in the late 1990s seems to have reached a stage where the author's persona is increasingly constructed as that of an 'elder' whose speech brooks no contradiction, however much aware it also is of the fact that 'being human and therefore limited and imperfect', readers' needs of such a persona cannot always be fulfilled.[34]

What, then, can a critic do? Having charted Walker's self-fashioning as victim/survivor, activist/teacher, writer/healer and finally elder through the non-fictional writings, my examination of the novels in the chapters which follow will both draw on and diverge from the author-itative course of explication she has set out in her essays. Taking that course as a starting point rather than the final word, I want to turn to two women whose work has shaped and informed Walker's writing throughout her career. Zora Neale Hurston and Virginia Woolf enable an understanding of Walker's writing above and beyond what 'influence' the author herself has acknowledged, and this is why a discussion of both may offer a way out of the critical vicious circle which has so far emerged in this chapter.

WALKER AND HURSTON

We are a people. A people do no throw their geniuses away.
And if they are thrown away, it is our duty as artists and as witnesses for the future to collect them again for the sake of our children, and, if necessary, bone by bone.[35]

This familiar quotation from 'Zora Neale Hurston: a Cautionary Tale and a Partisan View' is generally used to shore up Walker's claim to rediscovering Zora Neale Hurston in the early 1970s whilst doing research for her short story about voodoo, 'The Revenge of Hannah Kemhuff'. In the essay which follows it, 'Looking for Zora', Walker further recounts her attempt at recovering Hurston almost literally 'bone by bone' by visiting her burial place and marking it with a headstone proclaiming Hurston 'a genius of the South'. Walker's celebration of Hurston, however, is, as Diane Sadoff notes in 'Black Matrilineage: The Case of Walker and Hurston', not without anxiety and we can read this anxiety in the extract above, which brings various uncomfortable questions in its train. Will Walker's own work survive, or who is going to recollect it? What are the forces that conspired against Zora's survival, and to what extent do they still pertain in the culture's disrespect for black women's writing? Sad-off's answer is that Walker *needed* a literary foremother to validate her own writerly identity, she 'virtually invents Hurston before she defines herself as indebted to Hurston's example'.[36] That 'Anything We Love Can Be Saved' is Walker's own, much later rationalisation for the anxiety of loss, as if in saving Zora Neale Hurston's legacy for posterity she was also safeguarding her own. Hurston then is not only a role model and ancestor, but a legitimating presence for Walker in the African American literary tradition. In search of her mother's garden, Walker not only finds the creativity of the woman who gave birth to her; she also *fails* to find Zora's grave in the overgrown piece of land where it is supposed to be. The recollection, then, is by necessity a matter of conjecture or indeed invention; as Kadiatu Kanneh has said, 'Black cultures of resistance as well as Black self-recognitions are not always, or ever, *simply* inherited. Black/feminist identities, in order to gain a valid political voice, have repeatedly and contextually to reinvent themselves in dialogue and conflict with racism.'[37]

In Walker's fear of loss it is not just racism that is the problem, but also sexism and the failure of oppressed people, at times, to honour their own. Kanneh titles her essay 'Mixed Feelings: When My Mother's Garden is Unfamiliar' because she is concerned primarily with matrilineages which are broken because of migration or racial/cultural differences between mothers and children. The idea of a constructed, rather than simply inherited or found, matrilineage applies to the case of Walker and Hurston as well. Many have written about the similarities between the two; indeed, Lillie P. Howard has devoted a whole book to this literary coupling, yet I cannot help but feel that in this endeavour most critics simply follow Walker's lead rather than interrogate what her *interest* in Hurston actually might be.[38] If we chart the similarities first, they consist ostensibly in a joint commitment to Southern 'folk' culture and more especially the black vernacular; in the self-emancipation of black women like Hurston's Janie Crawford in *Their Eyes Were Watching God* and Walker's Celie; in the struggle, also, for a farmer's daughter like Walker and the granddaughter of a slave like Hurston to live by the word as self-respecting and respected black women intellectuals and writers. Similarities in the work—especially the parallels between *Their Eyes Were Watching God* and *The Color Purple*—are traced by critic after critic in article after article, and rightly put in the African American tradition of one writer's revision of another's work, or of signifying upon it. Yet few dare to ask, as Henry Louis Gates Jr does in 'Color Me Zora', where Hurston's presence in Walker's fiction is to be found other than in *The Color Purple*; as Michael Cooke observes, the two have interests in common but 'Walker operates on a different pitch and scale'.[39] That difference in tone is identified by Walker herself in an interview as Hurston's lightheartedness and optimism by contrast with her own thematics of black women's suffering and struggle. Again, with the exception of *The Color Purple*, Walker is earnest and serious where Hurston's prose is notoriously slippery and *slant* and plays tricks on its readers.[40] The question of Walker's interest or rather *investment* in Hurston is then only partially answered with a need for self-legitimation. Of all the parallels and shared interests cited, many are of Walker's own and conscious making (such as giving Celie the autonomous voice that Janie lacks in *Their Eyes Were Watching God*, due to its framing of the vernacular by the narrator's discourse), whereas others are of her choosing: Hurston's focus on black women is only evident in that one novel and much less prominent in her other texts; Hurston was a political conservative and cultural separatist, whereas Walker is the opposite, and so on. Yet I do think that folk culture and the black vernacular are what Walker 'sees in' Hurston and what she needs from her. Trudier Harris's comparison of some of Hurston and Walker's short stories put me on the trail of thinking about Walker's migration from the South and the distance she has travelled from family and cultural roots, a distance that her work constantly seeks to undo. Harris argues that Hurston and Walker do not occupy the same position when it comes to African American folk culture: '[it] is the difference between intimate knowledge of the culture as usually possessed by the insider, and acquaintance with the culture as usually possessed by those who are to some extent outside'.[41] Harris's point is that Walker uses Hurston to get back to her Southern roots, with varying degrees of success. In stories such as 'To Hell with Dying' it works, but in 'The Revenge of Hannah Kemhuff' and 'Strong Horse Tea' it does not, in Harris's view, because in those two stories Walker in effect discredits rootworking and conjuring. I mentioned earlier that 'The Revenge of Hannah Kemhuff' came out of a story that Walker's mother told her about an incident that happened to *her* mother during the Depression; Walker then went to research rootworking and found the anthropological work on voodoo *Mules and Men* (from which the story quotes the text of a curse collected by Hurston in the course of her research).[42] What this genealogy of the short story shows is Walker's need to verify, to legitimise her mother's discourse with reference to scholarly work; the delight Walker expresses in finding 'this perfect book' [*Mules and Men*] in a library is in large part due to the fact that another Southern black woman's scholarship—Hurston's—can indeed confirm the 'truth' of the first black Southern woman's private and domestic account of history. Something similar goes on in the story 'Everyday Use', where an educated daughter returns to the South to claim her mother's quilts as art, except in this story the narrator is clearly critical of such high-cultural validation (and appropriation) of an indigenous and *useful* folk practice.[43] The argument in 'Everyday Use' and the implication of the essay, where Walker relates her delight at discovering Hurston's legitimising book, are therefore at odds with each other. Still, it may well be that what Hurston, when Walker first 'recognised' her as a kindred spirit, enabled Walker to do is bridge the distance between her (by then) educated middle-class and predominantly Northern existence and the life of hard rural labour that was her parents' lot in the South. This desire for a 'cultural return' to the South is not unique, nor is it only a personal preoccupation on Walker's part. After all, she shares the experience of migration to the North with many African Americans this century and with many of her generation, who moved away for reasons of education and employment.

In a 1984 interview Walker said in so many words that the vernacular of *The Color Purple* represents a means of recovering Southern black culture:

> This was the way my grandparents spoke, this is the way my mother speaks today, and I want to capture that. Especially for my daughter, who has a very different kind of upbringing and who doesn't get to Georgia very often. I want her to know when she grows up what her grandparents, her great-grandparents, sounded like, because the sound is so amazingly alive.[44]

Celie's vernacular letters also link Walker's mother's speech with Hurston's achievement in *Their Eyes Were Watching God*, for as Walker explains in another interview, '[Zora] saw poetry where other writers saw merely failure to cope with English.'[45] Hurston, in short, binds the private world of Walker's family history and the public one of anthropology and the literary tradition together. The discovery of her work makes it possible for Walker to shift her activism from Civil Rights to teaching and writing without losing touch with Southern culture, at a time when she is geographically and in terms of class and education removed from it. But this is not the only tie that binds. Even more importantly, I think, Hurston's example enables Walker to articulate her critique of race and gender relations in the feminist post-Civil Rights era and to theorise it in the concept of womanism.

Walker's definition of womanism at the beginning of *In Search of Our Mothers' Gardens* presents less a political analysis of black women's oppression, let alone a programme to end it, than a depiction of a positive role model:

> **Womanist 1.** From *womanish*. (Opp. of 'girlish' i.e. frivolous, irresponsible, not serious.) A black feminist or feminist of color. [. . . .] Usually referring to outrageous, audacious, courageous or *willful* behavior. Wanting to know more and in greater depth than is considered 'good' for one. [. . . .] Responsible. In charge. *Serious.*

This first set of epithets for the womanist woman does three things: it invokes the black folk speech ('womanish') that Zora Neale Hurston liberated from its degraded status as defective English; it posits a model of black femininity which Hurston's lifestyle and demeanour embodied perfectly ('outrageous, audacious')—and which is in many ways antithetical to Walker's own; and it implicitly contrasts this black femininity with white feminism. In the bracketed reference to 'girlishness' Walker appeals to a notion prevalent in black feminism of the 1970s that white women's sense of their own oppression was like the cry of a spoilt child. Echoing Sojourner Truth, they felt that middle-class white women might protest against feminine passivity and agitate for their rights to paid employment and reproductive freedom, but that they should not be left in blissful ignorance of the active, hard-working lives that most American women (black and working class) led out of sheer necessity (in *Meridian* such resentment of white women as wide-eyed and un-serious is articulated by the protagonist herself). In the second section of Walker's definition of womanism this critique of 1970s white feminism continues:

> **2.** *Also*: A woman who loves other women, sexually and/or non-sexually. Appreciates and prefers women's culture, women's emotional flexibility . . . and women's strength. Sometimes loves individual men, sexually and/or non-sexually. Committed to survival whole of entire people, male and female. Not a separatist, except periodically, for health. Traditionally universalist [= aware of the fact that] 'the colored race is like a flower garden, with every color flower represented'. Traditionally capable [= leading slaves to escape to Canada]

This section draws both on Hurston's notion of African Americans' diversity and on white radical feminism's valorisation of woman-bonding and women's culture. But in its refusal of separatism—which can apply to racial and lesbian separatism—it revises both. Hurston is reputed to have been against the desegregation of schools in the 1950s, believing that racial health was most likely fostered by separate education, like her own upbringing in an all-black town. Feminist separatists of the 1970s believed that heterosexuality and feminism were incompatible, because to love men meant to 'sleep with the enemy'. Walker's definition refuses such separatism as an ideology but still leaves the door open for temporary autonomous organisation or—significantly—for the validity of Hurston's view as a strategic choice based upon experience. Significant also is Walker's emphasis on the 'traditionally' universalist and the 'traditionally' capable, which again can be read as targeting the naivety of white women's self-styled 'revolutionary' demand to be released from patriarchal bondage. Black women have always been 'revolutionaries', and black women have a long history of struggle against oppression. They have also always been aware of diversity within a common cause, and this lesson white women have yet to learn, Walker implies. The womanist is committed to both her gender and her race on preferential and historical grounds rather than those of biology, and she values the culture that history has given her:

> **3.** Loves music. Loves dance. Loves the moon. *Loves* the Spirit.
> . . . Loves struggle. Loves the Folk. Loves herself. *Regardless.*

Pleasure and sensuality are foregrounded here; womanism is articulated as a political identity which is integrated into everyday life, non-elitist, and positive/active rather than determined by victim-status. Again Zora, who loved the Folk, the Spirit and herself, serves as a model. Walker ends her definition with a clinching of her polemic with white feminists:

4. Womanist is to feminist as purple to lavender.[46]

Tuzyline Jita Allan, who has given the concept of womanism more theoretical attention than any other feminist critic, sees this last line in Walker's definition as divisive. 'Walker sets up (black) womanism and (white) feminism in a binary opposition from which the former emerges a privileged, original term and the latter, a devalued, pale replica', she argues.[47] I am not sure that this is quite right. American lesbian feminists took lavender as their colour in the 1970s, well before *The Color Purple* and *In Search of Our Mothers' Gardens*. Walker intensifies this colour, deepens and darkens it by mixing it with black; in this way she not so much rejects white feminism as absorbs it into her project and *radicalises* it to the point of no return. Allan's charge that womanism is an essentialist notion because it pertains to 'black feminists and feminists of color' and thus excludes white women, may seem valid at first but is not, if we read womanism as subsuming (white) feminism in this way.[48] Within the larger scheme of the essays in *In Search of Our Mothers' Gardens* and of the later novels, where Walker frequently revises white feminism for her own purposes, there is much more scope for feminist/womanist integration than it might at first appear. And this makes sense, not only because of Walker's allegiance to the Civil Rights ethos of 'black and white together' but also because her brand of spiritual universalism embraces all who are aware of their hybrid natures—including white women.

If, then, Walker needed Zora Neale Hurston to formulate womanism as a radicalisation of (white) feminist analysis and aspiration, that analysis itself would have had to be in place as a necessary pre-condition for Walker's critique and revision of it. The Women's Liberation movement of the late 1960s and 70s provided such an analysis, for example in Kate Millett's bestseller *Sexual Politics*—but Millett is never mentioned in Alice Walker's work. It seems that Walker's polemic with white feminism was primarily conducted as a *literary* activism on behalf of African American women's writing, and for that purpose Walker built on the work of Virginia Woolf.

WALKER AND WOOLF

Recently, I read at a college and was asked by one of the audience what I considered the major difference between the literature written by black and by white Americans. I had not spent a lot of time considering this question, since it is not the difference between them that interests me, but, rather, the way that black writers and white writers seem to me to be writing one immense story—the same story, for the most part—with different parts of this immense story coming from a multitude of different perspectives. Until this is generally recognized, literature will always be broken into bits, black and white, and there will always be questions, wanting neat answers, such as this.[49]

By comparison with Hurston, Alice Walker's debt to Virginia Woolf is relatively little acknowledged, either by herself or by the critics who engage with her work. Walker mentions Woolf on two occasions: first in 'Saving the Life That Is Your Own', amongst other writers who have served as models for her, adding that Woolf 'saved so many of us', and second in *The Same River Twice*, where she explains that Olivia in *The Color Purple* was not named after Oliver Twist but for the Olivia of that famous closet-lesbian line 'Chloe liked Olivia' in *A Room of One's Own*, 'a book that made me happy to be a writer, and bolstered and brightened my consciousness about the role other women, often silenced or even long dead, can have in changing the world'.[50] *A Room of One's Own* must indeed have been a key text for Walker, because there Virginia Woolf famously wrote, in the passage that leads up to the one about 'a woman's sentence':

> they [women] had no tradition behind them, or one so short and partial that it was of little help. For we think back through our mothers if we are women. It is useless to go to the great men writers for help, however much one may go to them for pleasure.[51]

The search for predecessors was rather more fruitful for Woolf than it was for Walker; after all, Woolf could choose from a long and relatively continuous line of writing women in the (white) European tradition from medieval times onwards. When Walker takes Woolf at her word and thinks back through her Southern black mother and her Native American grandmother, she finds a long and relatively continuous line of non-writers, illiterate women burdened with domestic and wage-labour, to whom the world of literature was either unknown or barely conceivable. 'How was the creativity of the black woman kept alive, year after year and century after century, when for most of the years black people have been in America, it was a punishable crime for a black person to read or write?' Walker asks pertinently.[52] Other than Phillis Wheatley, the slave who in 1773 had her *Poems* published (anonymously) in London, and a handful of other black women writers—Zora Neale Hurston among them—as well as important

role models like Jean Toomer, James Baldwin and Langston Hughes, Walker
was left to her own devices. She argues, in her critical revision of *A Room of
One's Own*, that artists of another kind (quiltmakers, weavers, cooks, African
hut-painters, gardeners, and last but not least storytellers) were the
Shakespeare's sisters of the African American tradition. Extrapolating from
Woolf's statement that 'Anon, who wrote so many poems without signing
them, was often a woman', she concludes: 'And so our mothers and
grandmothers have, more often than not anonymously, handed on the
creative spark, the seed of the flower they themselves never hoped to see: or
like a sealed letter they could not plainly read.'[53] This reference to the sealed
letter is reminiscent of *The Color Purple*, where Celie for a long time cannot
read Nettie's sealed letters after Mr has confiscated them, but there is
another resonance here too: with Hurston, whose writing Walker could not
read due to the intervention of a racist and patriarchal literary institution
which failed to honour her work. Apart from these unwitting allusions to her
own later novels, Walker's use of Woolf here also makes visible the class and
racial limitations of Woolf's argument and exposes white feminism's
universalist assumption that all women share the concerns of the educated
white middle class. Still, since Walker needs Woolf to make this clear, the
question arises whether it is possible to forge an interracial tradition of
women's writing despite these differences. The relative silence which
surrounds the Walker/Woolf nexus in feminist criticism might suggest that
it is not; to date, the domains of Woolf criticism and of African American
criticism remain largely segregated. White women write of Woolf, at great
length and in great quantity, while black feminist critics focus their attention
over-whelmingly on African American writing. The one exception I know of,
Tuzyline Jita Allan, reads *Mrs Dalloway* and other white women's texts by
Walker's womanist lights to productive critical effect, but she is indeed an
exception: both black and white feminist critics, however wise they are to the
mechanisms of binary logic and essentialist thinking, have tended to stick to
(what they see as) their own. Writing itself however, as Alice Walker says in
the opening statement to this section, does not work exclusively along lines
of racial (or gender) identification in this way, nor can it afford to. Reading
does not work in this way either. How, then, can thinking about the relation
between Walker and Woolf contribute to the construction of a literary
tradition which more accurately reflects 'the immense story' of which Walker
feels her work, and that of Woolf, is a part? Recent debates about canon
formation tend to recognise—however fraught they may otherwise be—that
a segregated canon is unsatisfactory. Walker herself acknowledges this when
she writes that she always felt she needed to read Hurston *and* Flannery
O'Connor, Nella Larsen *and* Carson McCullers, Jean Toomer *and* William
Faulkner in order to even begin to feel well educated at all.[54] Yet the danger

is, if we are not to read Walker's work purely in terms of 'the' African American tradition as is usually done, but to put it in dialogue with white writers like Woolf, that we may be assuming an indebtedness which is misplaced. Walker herself is the chief consciousness-raiser of this phenomenon: '[T]his is what has happened to black culture all these years: We produce and produce and create and create and it finds its way into mainstream culture ten years later, white people assuming they are the source of it.'[55] The 'immense story' that black and white writers are evidently piecing together like a quilt, may be a collective and colourful story 'coming from a multitude of different perspectives', but it does not get written in any idealised setting of sisterly equality and collaboration. In the context of literary institutions such as prizes, educational establishments, canon formations and the publishing industry, writers and artists compete for recognition and—indeed—ownership of ideas and creative practices. In thinking about Woolf as one of Alice Walker's ancestors or foremothers, the 'assumption that whites are at the source of it' would seem to be reproduced. Or maybe not. It may be, as I think Walker is trying to say in her statement on the difference between black and white writers, that what parts of the 'immense story' already exist and are legible as 'mainstream' are therefore also available for revision, appropriation and unexpected identifications on the part of their readers. Walker's work lends itself—some might say all too easily—to interracial reading; the black and white feminist criticism which her work has generated testifies to this. Conversely, it is quite conceivable that black women like Walker might have read *A Room of One's Own* or *Three Guineas* at Spelman College in the 1960s, before the flowering of black women's writing as we know it today had come into being. They might indeed have felt alienated by it, but they might equally well have 'recognised' Spelman in Woolf's depiction of Newnham and Girton, and they might have cheered Woolf's pacifist stance in the light of the Civil Rights movement and protests against the Vietnam War, less on the grounds of gender *per se* than on those of race.

Woolf's polemical work, in other words, is productive for African American writers like Alice Walker, whilst at the same time our engagement with Walker illuminates Woolf, highlighting gaps in gender analysis as well as the racist assumptions which are embedded in the latter's critique of empire and colonialism.

Reading Walker with Woolf, as with Hurston, can raise our consciousness about what is involved when 'our mother's garden is unfamiliar'. Most obviously, it makes visible those places in Woolf's work where 'race' surfaces, places which usually are overlooked, regarded as insignificant or politely acknowledged as (historically excusable) instances of Woolf's blindness to what is now acknowledged to be just as important a category of historical silencing as gender is. What Toni Morrison calls a search for 'the ghost in the machine', black women's presence in the white woman's text, yields examples like the Moor on the first page of *Orlando*; the mysterious black woman on the beach in *Jacob's Room*; and most startling of all, 'a very fine negress' in *A Room of One's Own*.[56] In the middle of a meditation on women writers' anonymity over the centuries, and their tendency to make themselves invisible for fear of opprobrium, Woolf writes:

> They [women] are not even now as concerned about the health of their fame as men are, and, speaking generally, will pass a tombstone or a signpost without feeling an irresistible desire to cut their names on it, as Alf, Bert or Chas. must do in obedience to their instinct, which murmurs if it sees a fine woman go by, or even a dog, Ce chien est à moi. And, of course, it may not be a dog, I thought, remembering Parliament Square, the Sieges Allee and other avenues; it may be a piece of land or a man with black curly hair. It is one of the great advantages of being a woman that one can pass even a very fine negress without wishing to make an Englishwoman of her.
>
> That woman, then, who was born with a gift of poetry in the sixteenth century . . . [57]

(That is an awkward break, I thought when I first read this. It is upsetting to come upon 'a very fine negress' all of a sudden. The continuity is disturbed. One might say, I continued, laying the book down beside *In Search of Our Mothers' Gardens*, that the woman who wrote those pages had more genius in her than Jane Austen, but if one reads them over and marks that jerk in them, that condescension and complacency, one sees that she will never get her genius expressed whole and entire. Her books will be deformed and twisted. She will write blindly where she should have her eyes wide open. She will write patronisingly where she should write critically. She will write of herself where she should write of other women. She is at odds with her sisters. How could she help but die middle-aged, cramped and thwarted?)

If I were a polemicist like Virginia Woolf, or Alice Walker, this is what I would say. Reading them in dialogue with each other we see a peculiar argument in Woolf's gender-based critique of colonialism: the Englishwoman does not wish to make the negress over in her own image, presumably like men want to do with the man with black curly hair, 'civilise him'. But what does she want, then? To leave the negress as she is, a 'very fine' specimen of nature to be gawped at in the street? Or merely to acknowledge cultural difference, without ever even thinking that the black woman is also a woman, and might—indeed—be an Englishwoman as well? The passage is reminiscent of *Three Guineas*, where Woolf similarly disavows (white) women's share in, and responsibility for, the legacy of empire. When writing of the woman as outsider to all the institutions of Englishness, Woolf impersonates the 'educated man's daughter' to interrogate patriarchal and patriotic ideology:

> 'Our country', she will say, 'throughout the greater part of its history has treated me as a slave; it has denied me education or a share in its possessions. 'Our' country still ceases to be mine if I marry a foreigner.[. . .] 'For', the outsider will say, 'in fact, as a woman, I have no country. As a woman I want no country. As a woman my country is the whole world.'[58]

This statement of Woolf's feminist internationalism is as inclusive and inoffensive as Alice Walker's 'immense story' being written by black and white together, and it obscures differential relations of power in the same way. Woolf's intended solidarity with women all over the world sounds hollow in the light of what we now know about the difficulties of forging a global sisterhood, and we know it in part through the efforts of an Alice Walker, Toni Morrison or the African American critics of more recent vintage, whose internationalism is of a different kind.[59] Walker revises Woolf in this sense in the essay '*One* Child of One's Own', where she writes boldly

> Of the need for internationalism, alignment with non-Americans, non-Europeans and non-chauvinists and again male supremacists or white supremacists wherever they exist on the globe, with an appreciation of all white American feminists who know more of nonwhite women's herstory than 'And Ain't I a Woman' by Sojourner Truth.[60]

Race *and* gender are inscribed here in a more sophisticated global alliance than Woolf proposed, because of Walker's rejection, in the last line, of a rigid identity politics. Her 'appreciation' of white women's self-education about cultural difference echoes Woolf's insistence on women's self-education about gender and literary ancestry, and it invalidates Tuzyline Allan's charge of womanist essentialism in the process.

The picture which emerges is that Walker and Woolf are, in fact, remarkably similar writers. Both wrote in a variety of different forms, ranging from journalism (the *Times Literary Supplement*; *Ms* magazine), novels and essays to biographies of men they admired (Langston Hughes and Roger Fry), diaries and letters. They share the concern not to be confined to a gender- or race-segregated readership *precisely because* of their race and gender critiques. Furthermore, because both feel at home in different forms, they are able to parody or stretch those forms in order to highlight modes of discursive power embedded within, for example, conventional biography (which Woolf satirised in *Jacob's Room* and *Orlando*) or the English epistolary novel (which Walker parodies in *The Color Purple*). This manipulation of form in the service of a race and gender critique is especially effective in Woolf's and Walker's essays, where an often chatty and narrative style (wandering on and off the garden path, as in *A Room of One's Own*) disguises a complex and sophisticated argument. And because this argument is not authoritatively laid down as linear logic, the essay-as-story draws us unsuspecting readers in, turns our heads and by such distraction gets us to exactly the place where Woolf and Walker want to have us. The essays, in other words, are just as much works of creative writing as any of the novels or short fiction, and in Walker's case short stories such as 'Nineteen Fifty-Five' and 'Advancing Luna—and Ida B. Wells' are in turn every bit as critical and argumentative as any of her more overtly political essays.

Thematic parallels derive from such formal similarities. 'Madness' engendered by societal constraints around gender and race is found in the work of both authors (*Mrs Dalloway, Meridian, The Voyage Out, Possessing the Secret of Joy*); critiques of official (that is: male or white Western) historiography and biography, particularly with regard to empire and war, can be read in *Between the Acts, Orlando*, and *Jacob's Room* but also in *Meridian* and *The Temple of My Familiar*. Perhaps most strikingly of all, both writers use the family saga to expose the taboo of domestic violence and child abuse (emotional as well as sexual) in *The Years, The Color Purple, To the Lighthouse* (albeit in very muted form) and *The Third Life of Grange Copeland*. Charting the transition to modernity, both *The Years* and *The Third Life of Grange Copeland* examine the interplay of individual and social histories through the crucible of successive generations of one family living, and being lived by, those histories.

In 'Unspeakable Things Unspoken' Toni Morrison warns against comparisons between African American and white writers,

> because comparisons are a major form of knowledge and flattery. The risks, nevertheless, are twofold: 1) the gathering of a culture's difference into the skirts of the Queen is a neutralization designed and constituted to elevate and maintain hegemony. 2) circum-scribing and limiting the literature to a mere reaction to or denial of the Queen, judging the work solely in terms of its reference to Eurocentric criteria, or its sociological accuracy, political correctness or its pretense of having no politics at all, cripple the literature and infantilize the serious work of imaginative writing. [. . . .] Finding or imposing Western influences in/on African-American literature has value, but where its sole purpose is to *place* value only where that influence is located is pernicious.[61]

Heeding Morrison's warning, and Walker's about white appropriation of black culture, should not mean that a comparison such as I have made between Walker and Woolf is ruled out of court. It provides indeed 'a form of knowledge', the more so because putting Walker and Woolf in dialogue with each other works to suggest different readings of both. In fact, such a comparison can demonstrate that—to cite Morrison once more: 'We are not, in fact, "other". We are choices. And to read imaginative literature by and about us is to choose to examine centers of the self and to have the opportunity to compare these centers with the "raceless" one with which we are, all of us, most familiar.'[62] Morrison's 'we', of course, refers to African Americans rather than black and white writers together, but it works for an interracial tradition too. Reading Woolf with Walker and Hurston defamiliarises the 'us' of a white feminism, which can no longer simply assume itself to be the preferred implied reader of 'women's' writing. Along parallel lines, reading Walker with Woolf shows how 'books continue each other' in a literary tradition which is neither entirely male and Eurocentric nor exclusively female or African American. Walker and Woolf and Morrison and Hurston create cultural spaces where few or none has gone before, and juxtaposing them opens up the space of 'a culture's difference' in the very act of ostensibly closing it.

One final example may illustrate this. In *The Same River Twice* Walker recounts her experience working with Steven Spielberg on the set of *The Color Purple*. Spielberg asks her to appear in the film, their film, holding his young son Max. Walker refuses:

> of course I could not. There is just too much history for that to have been possible. It's a very long Southern/South African tradition, after all—black women holding white babies. And yet I felt so sad for us all, that this should be so. And especially moved by you [Spielberg], who had this history as no part of your consciousness.[63]

There are comparisons to be made *and* there are differences to be articulated; the relationships between black women and white babies, black writers and white foremothers, are problematic and difficult—and all the more worthwhile for that. They are one place where different patches of the 'immense story' are stitched together.

NOTES

1. John O'Brien, 'Alice Walker: an Interview' [1973], in Henry Louis Gates Jr and K. A. Appiah (eds), *Alice Walker: Critical Perspectives Past and Present* (New York: Amistad, 1993), p. 331.

2. Ibid.
3. Ruth-Ellen Boetcher Joeres and Elizabeth Mittman, 'An Introductory Essay', in Ruth-Ellen Boetcher Joeres and Elizabeth Mittman (eds), *The Politics of the Essay: Feminist Perspectives* (Bloomington: Indiana University Press, 1993), p. 16.
4. Roland Barthes, 'The Death of the Author' [1968], in Philip Rice and Patricia Waugh (eds), Modern Literary Theory: a Reader, second edition (London: Edward Arnold, 1992), pp. 114–18.
5. Sharon Wilson, 'An Interview with Alice Walker' [1984], in Gates and Appiah (eds), *Alice Walker*, p. 319.
6. Alice Walker, 'The Black Writer and the Southern Experience' [1970], in *In Search of Our Mothers' Gardens: Womanist Prose* (London: Women's Press, 1984), p. 17.
7. Ibid., p. 21.
8. Alice Walker, 'Saving the Life That Is Your Own: The Importance of Models in the Artist's Life', in *In Search of Our Mothers' Gardens*, pp. 3–14; 'The Old Artist: Notes on Mr Sweet', in *Living by the Word: Selected Writings 1973–1987* (London: Women's Press, 1988), p. 38. 'The Revenge of Hannah Kemhuff' and 'To Hell with Dying' are published in Alice Walker, *In Love and Trouble: Stories of Black Women* [1973] (London: Women's Press, 1984).
9. Alice Walker, 'Beauty: When the Other Dancer Is the Self' [1984], in *In Search of Our Mothers' Gardens*, p. 386.
10. Ibid., p. 393.
11. O'Brien, 'Alice Walker: an Interview', p. 327.
12. Alice Walker, 'The Unglamorous But Worthwhile Duties of the Black Revolutionary Artist, or of the Black Writer Who Simply Works and Writes' [1971], in *In Search of Our Mothers' Gardens*, p. 130.
13. O'Brien, 'Alice Walker: an Interview', p. 330.
14. Ibid., p. 329.
15. Alice Walker, 'The Civil Rights Movement: What Good Was It?' [1967], in *In Search of Our Mothers' Gardens*, p. 125.
16. Alice Walker, ' "But Yet and Still the Cotton Gin Kept on Working . . ." ' [1970], in *In Search of Our Mothers' Gardens*, p. 28.
17. Alice Walker, 'Breaking Chains and Encouraging Life' [1980], in *In Search of Our Mothers' Gardens*, pp. 287–8.
18. Alice Walker, '*One* Child of One's Own' [1979], in *In Search of Our Mothers' Gardens*, p. 367.
19. O'Brien, 'Alice Walker: an Interview', p. 337.
20. Walker, '*One* Child of One's Own', p. 372.
21. Alice Walker, 'Writing *The Color Purple*' [1982], in *In Search of Our Mothers' Gardens*, p. 357.
22. Alice Walker, 'Coming in from the Cold: Welcoming the Old, Funny-talking Ancient Ones into the Warm Room of Present Consciousness, or,

Natty Dread Rides Again!' [1984], in *Living by the Word*, p. 55.

23. Alice Walker, 'In the Closet of the Soul' [1987], in *Living by the Word*, p. 79.

24. Ibid., p. 82.

25. Ibid., p. 87.

26. O'Brien, 'Alice Walker: an Interview', p. 332.

27. Alice Walker, 'The Only Reason You Want to Go to Heaven Is That You Have Been Driven Out of Your Mind (Off Your Land and Out of Your Lover's Arms): Clear Seeing Inherited Religion and the Pagan Self' [*sic*], in *Anything We Love Can Be Saved: A Writer's Activism* (London: Women's Press, 1997), p. 17.

28. Miller's whole *oeuvre* focuses on various forms of child abuse; see, for example, *The Untouched Key: Tracing Childhood Trauma in Creativity and Destructiveness* (London: Virago, 1990) and *Banished Knowledge: Facing Childhood Injuries* (London: Virago, 1991).

29. Alice Walker, '"You All Have Seen": If the Women of the World Were Comfortable, This Would be a Comfortable World', in *Anything We Love Can Be Saved, p. 31.*

30. Alice Walker, 'A Letter to President Clinton' [1996], in *Anything We Love Can Be Saved*, p. 209.

31. Ibid.

32. Wilson, 'An Interview with Alice Walker', p. 320.

33. Alice Walker, 'Getting as Black as My Daddy: Thoughts on the Unhelpful Aspects of Destructive Criticism', in *Anything We Love Can Be Saved, p. 151.*

34. Alice Walker, 'This That I Offer You: People Get Tired; Sometimes They Have Other Things to Do', in *Anything We Love Can Be Saved*, p. 177.

35. Alice Walker, 'Zora Neale Hurston: a Cautionary Tale and a Partisan View' [1979], in *In Search of Our Mothers' Gardens*, p. 92.

36. Diane Sadoff, 'Black Matrilineage: The Case of Walker and Hurston', in Harold Bloom (ed.), *Alice Walker*, Modern Critical Views (New York: Chelsea House, 1989), p. 118.

37. Kadiatu Kanneh, 'Mixed Feelings: When My Mother's Garden is Unfamiliar', in Sally Ledger, Josephine McDonagh and Jane Spencer (eds), *Political Gender: Texts and Contexts* (London: Harvester Wheat-sheaf, 1994), p. 36.

38. Lillie P. Howard (ed.), *Alice Walker and Zora Neale Hurston: the Common Bond* (London: Greenwood Press, 1993); Molly Hite, 'Romance, Marginality and Matrilineage: *The Color Purple* and *Their Eyes Were Watching God*', in Henry Louis Gates Jr (ed.), *Reading Black, Reading Feminist: a Critical Anthology* (New York: Meridian, 1990), pp. 431–54; Henry Louis Gates Jr, 'Color Me Zora', in Gates and Appiah (eds), *Alice Walker*, pp. 239–60.

39. Gates, 'Color Me Zora', p. 244; Michael Cooke, *Afro-American Literature in the Twentieth Century: the Achievement of Intimacy* (London: Yale University Press, 1984), p. 34.

40. Wilson, 'An Interview with Alice Walker', p. 324.

41. Trudier Harris, 'Our People, Our People', in Howard (ed.), *Alice Walker and Zora Neale Hurston*, p. 32.

42. Alice Walker, 'Saving the Life That Is Your Own: the Importance of Models in the Artist's Life' [1976], in *In Search of Our Mothers' Gardens*, p. 11.

43. Alice Walker, 'Everyday Use', in *In Love and Trouble*, pp. 47–59.

44. Wilson, 'An Interview with Alice Walker', p. 320.

45. O'Brien, 'Alice Walker: an Interview', p. 338.

46. Alice Walker, *In Search of Our Mothers' Gardens*, pp. xi–xii.

47. Tuzyline Jita Allan, *Womanist & Feminist Aesthetics: A Comparative Review* (Athens: Ohio University Press, 1995), p. 6.

48. Ibid., p. 93.

49. Walker, 'Saving the Life That Is Your Own', p. 5.

50. Ibid., p. 14; Alice Walker, 'The River: Honoring the Difficult', in *The Same River Twice*, p. 41.

51. Virginia Woolf, *A Room of One's Own* (New York: Harcourt Brace Jovanovich, 1927), p. 79.

52. Alice Walker, 'In Search of Our Mothers' Gardens' [1974], in *In Search of Our Mothers' Gardens*, p. 234.

53. Ibid., p. 240.

54. Alice Walker, 'Beyond the Peacock: the Reconstruction of Flannery O'Connor' [1975], in *In Search of Our Mothers' Gardens*, p. 43.

55. Alice Walker, 'Alice Walker on the Movie The Color Purple', in *The Same River Twice*, p. 203.

56. Toni Morrison, 'Unspeakable Things Unspoken: the Afro-American Presence in American Literature', *Michigan Quarterly Review* (Winter 1988), p. 11.

57. Woolf, *A Room of One's Own*, p. 52.

58. Virginia Woolf, *Three Guineas* [1938] (Harmondsworth: Penguin, 1977), p. 125.

59. For this kind of internationalism, see, for example, Patricia Hill Collins, Black Feminist Thought: Knowledge, Consciousness, and the Politics of Empowerment (London: Routledge, 1991); Carole Boyce Davies, *Black Women, Writing and Identity: Migrations of the Subject* (London: Routledge, 1994) and the two volumes of *Moving Beyond Boundaries*: vol. 1, Carole Boyce Davies and 'Molara Ogundipe-Leslie (eds), *International Dimensions of Black Women's Writing* (London: Pluto, 1995), and vol. 2, Carole Boyce Davies (ed.), *Black Women's Diasporas* (London: Pluto, 1995).

60. Walker, 'One Child of One's Own', p. 378.

61. Morrison, 'Unspeakable Things Unspoken', p. 10.

62. Ibid., p. 9.

63. Alice Walker, 'Deep Waters', in *The Same River Twice*, p. 216.

HENRY LOUIS GATES, JR.

Color Me Zora: Alice Walker's (Re) Writing of the Speakerly Text

O, write my name, O write my name:
      O write my name . . .
Write my name when-a you get home . . .
Yes, write my name in the book of life . . .
The Angels in the heav'n going-to write my name.
         Spiritual Underground Railroad

My spirit leans in joyousness tow'rd thine,
My gifted sister, as with gladdened heart
My vision flies along thy "speaking pages."
      Ada, "A Young Woman of Color," 1836

    I am only a pen in His hand.
          Rebecca Cox Jackson

I'm just a link in a chain.
      Aretha Franklin, "Chain of Fools"

For just over two hundred years, the concern to depict the quest of the black speaking subject to find his or her voice has been a repeated topos of the black tradition, and perhaps has been its most central trope. As theme, as revised trope, as a double-voiced narrative strategy, the representation of

From *The Signifying Monkey: A Theory of African-American Literary Criticism* by Henry Louis Gates, Jr. Published by Oxford University Press, © 1988 by Henry Louis Gates, Jr. Reprinted by permission.

characters and texts finding a voice has functioned as a sign both of the formal unity of the Afro-American literary tradition and of the integrity of the black subjects depicted in this literature.

Esu's double voice and the language of Signifyin(g) have served throughout this book as unifying metaphors, indigenous to the tradition, both for patterns of revision from text to text and for modes of figuration at work within the text. The Anglo-African narrators published between 1770 and 1815 placed themselves in a line of descent through the successive revision of one trope, of a sacred text that refuses to speak to its would-be black auditor. In *Their Eyes Were Watching God*, Zora Neale Hurston depicts her protagonist's ultimate moment of self-awareness in her ability to name her own divided consciousness. As an element of theme and as a highly accomplished rhetorical strategy that depends for its effect on the bivocality of free indirect discourse, this voicing of a divided consciousness (another topos of the tradition) has been transformed in Ishmael Reed's *Mumbo Jumbo* into a remarkably self-reflexive representation of the ironies of writing a text in which two foregrounded voices compete with each other for control of narration itself. Whereas the development of the tradition to the publication of *Their Eyes Were Watching God* seems to have been preoccupied with the mimetic possibilities of the speaking voice, black fiction after *Their Eyes* would seem even more concerned to explore the implications of doubled voices upon strategies of writing.

Strategies as effective as Hurston's innovative use of free indirect discourse and Reed's bifurcated narrative voice lead one to wonder how a rhetorical strategy could possibly extend, or. Signify upon, the notions of voice at play in these major texts of the black tradition. How could a text possibly trope the extended strategies of voicing which we have seen to be in evidence in: *Their Eyes* and in *Mumbo Jumbo*? To Signify upon both Hurston's and Reed's strategies of narration would seem to demand a form of the novel that, at once, breaks with tradition yet revises the most salient features through which I have been defining the formal unity of this tradition.

Just as Hurston's and Reed's texts present seemingly immovable obstacles to an equally telling revision of the tradition's trope of voicing, so too does *Invisible Man*, the tradition's text of blackness and, in my opinion, its most profound achievement in the novel. The first-person narration of *Invisible Man*, the valorization of oral narration in *Their Eyes*, and the italicized interface of showing and telling in *Mumbo Jumbo*, taken together, would seem to leave rather little space in which narrative innovation could even possibly be attempted. Alice Walker's revisions of *Their Eyes Were Watching God* and of Rebecca Cox Jackson's *Gifts of Power*, however, have defined an entirely new mode of representation of the black quest to make the text speak.

To begin to account for the Signifyin(g) revisions at work in Walker's *The Color Purple*, it is useful to recall the dream of literacy figured in John Jea's autobiography. In Chapter 4, I maintained that Jea's odd revision of the scene of the Talking Book served to erase the figurative potential of this trope for the slave narrators who followed him. After Jea, slave narrators refigured a repeated scene of instruction in terms of reading and writing rather than in terms of making the text speak. While these two tropes are obviously related, it seems equally obvious that the latter represents a key reworking of the former, in terms more conducive to the directly polemical role in which the slave narratives were engaged in an antebellum America seemingly preoccupied with the future of human slavery.

While the trope of the Talking Book disappeared from the male slave narratives after Jea literalized it it is refigured in the mystical writings of Rebecca Cox Jackson, an Afro-American visionary and Shaker eldress who was a contemporary of Jea's. Jackson was a free black woman who lived between 1795 and 1871. She was a fascinating religious leader and feminist, who founded a Shaker sisterhood in Philadelphia in 1857, after a difficult struggle with her family, with her initial religious denomination, and even with the Shakers. Her extensive autobiographical writings (1830–1864) were collected and edited by Jean McMahon Humez, published in 1981, and reviewed by Alice Walker in that same year.[1] The reconstitution of Jackson's texts is one of the major scholarly achievements in Afro-American literature, both because of the richness of her texts and because the writings of black women in antebellum America are painfully scarce, especially when compared to the large body of writings by black men.

Jackson, like her contemporary black ex-slave writers, gives a prominent place in her texts to her own literacy training. Hers is a divinely inspired literacy training even more remarkable than Jea's. Writing between 1830 and 1832, just fifteen-odd years after Jea, Jackson–with or without Jea's text in mind–refigures Jea's divine scene of instruction. Jackson's refiguration of this supernatural event, however, is cast within a sexual opposition between male and female. Whereas her antecedents used the trope to define the initial sense of difference between slave and free, African and European, Jackson's revision charts the liberation of a (black) woman from a (black) man over the letter of the text. I bracket *black* because, as we shall see, Jackson freed herself of her brother's domination of her literacy and her ability to interpret, but supplanted him with a mythical white male interpreter.

Jackson, recalling Jea, writes, "After I received the blessing of God, I had a great desire to read the Bible." Lamenting the fact that "I am the only child of my mother that had not learning," she seeks out her brother to "give me one hour's lesson at night after supper or before we went to bed."[2] Her brother, a prominent clergyman in the Bethel African Methodist Episcopal

Church, was often "so tired when he would come home that he had not [the] power so to do," a situation, Jackson tells us, which would "grieve" her. But the situation that grieved Jackson even more was her brother's penchant to "rewrite" her words, to revise her dictation, one supposes, to make them more "presentable." Jackson takes great care to describe her frustration in the fight with her brother to control her flow of words:

> So I went to get my brother to write my letters and to read them. . . . I told him what to put in. Then I asked him to read. He did. I said, "Thee has put in more than I told thee." This he done several times. I then said, "I don't want thee to *word* my letter. In only want thee to write it." Then he said, "Sister, thee is the hardest one I ever wrote for!" These words, together with the manner that he had wrote my letter, pierced my soul like a sword. . . . I could not keep from crying.[3]

This scene is an uncanny prefigurement of the battle over her public speaking voice that Janie wages with Joe Starks in *Their Eyes Were Watching God*, as we have seen in Chapter 5. Jackson's brother, "tired" from his arduous work for the Lord, cannot be relied on to train his sister to read. When she compromises by asking him to serve as her amanuensis, he "words" her letters, as Jackson puts it, rather than simply translating her words (in their correct order, as narrated) from spoken to written form. This contest over her wording is not merely the anxiety the author experiences when edited or rewritten; rather, we eventually learn that Rebecca's rather individual mode of belief not only comes to threaten the minister-brother but also leads ultimately to a severance of the kinship bond. The brother-sister conflict over the "word" of the letter, then, prefigures an even more profound conflict over the word and letter of God's will.

God, however, takes sides. He comforts the grieving Rebecca with a divine message: "And these words were spoken in my heart, 'Be faithful, and the time shall come when you can write.' These words were spoken in my heart as though a tender father spoke them. My tears were gone in a moment."[4] God was as good as his promise. Just as he had done for his servant, John Jea, the Lord taught Jackson how to read:

> One day I was sitting finishing a dress in haste and in prayer [Jackson sustained herself by dressmaking.] This word was spoken in my mind, "Who learned the first man on earth?" "Why, God." "He is unchangeable, and if He learned the first man to read, He can learn you." I laid down my dress, picked up my Bible, ran upstairs, opened it, and kneeled down with it pressed to my breast, prayed earnestly to Almighty God if it was consisting to His holy will, to learn me to read His holy word.

And when I looked on the word, I began to read. And when I found I was reading, I was frightened–then I could not read one word. I closed my eyes again in prayer and then opened my eyes, began to read. So I done, until I read the chapter. . . . So I tried, took my Bible daily and praying and read until I could read anywhere. The first chapter that I read I never could know it after that day. I only knowed it was in James, but what chapter I can never tell.[5]

When confronted with the news, Jackson's incredulous husband challenged her claim: "Woman, you are agoing crazy!" Jackson, undaunted, read to him. "Down I sat and read through. And it was in James. So Samuel praised the Lord with me." Similarly, her brother accused her merely of memorizing passages overheard being read by his children: "Once thee has heard the children read, till thee has got it by heart." Once convinced by Jackson's husband, Jackson tells us with an air of triumph, "He sat down very sorrowful."

When challenged by her doubting brother, Jackson tells us, "I did not speak," allowing her husband, Samuel, to speak in her defense. At the end of her long description of this miracle of literacy, this "gift of power," she summarizes the event as "this unspeakable gift of Almighty God to me." It is this double representation of unspeakability which connects Jackson's miracle of literacy to Alice Walker's strategies of narration in *The Color Purple*.

Despite the parallel in Jackson's mini-narrative of her fight to control her words and Janie's fight to control hers (resolved, for Jackson, by the divine discourse of God, and for Janie by the black vernacular discourse of Signifyin(g), we know that Hurston did not have access to Jackson's texts. Walker, however, makes much of this scene in her essay on Jackson, underscoring the fact that "Jackson *was* taught to read and write by the spirit within her."[6] When Walker dedicates *The Color Purple* "To the Spirit," it is to this spirit which taught Rebecca Jackson to read. It is the representation of the unfolding of this gift of the "spirit within her," an "unspeakable gift," through which Walker represents the thoroughly dynamic development of her protagonist's consciousness, within the "unspeakable" medium of an epistolary novel comprised of letters written but never said, indeed written but never read. Celie's only reader, and Rebecca's only literacy teacher, is God.

Rather than representing the name of God as unspeakable, Walker represents Celie's words, her letters addressed to "God," as unspeakable. God is Celie's silent auditor, the addressee of most of her letters, written but never sent. This device, as Robert Stepto has suggested to me, is an echo of the first line of W. E. B. Du Bois's well-known "After-Thought" to *The Souls of Black Folk:* "Hear my cry, O God the Reader." But more important to our analysis of Walker's revisions of *Their Eyes Were Watching God*, Celie's written voice to God, her reader, tropes the written yet never uttered voice of free indirect discourse which is the predominant vehicle of narrative commentary in Hurston's novel.

As I have attempted to show in Chapter 5, Hurston draws upon free indirect discourse as a written voice masked as a speakerly voice, as an "oral hieroglyphic," as Hurston put it. Celie's voice in *The Color Purple*, on the other hand, is a spoken or mimetic voice, cast in dialect, yet marked as a written one–a mimetic voice masking as a diegetic voice, but also a diegetic voice masking as a mimetic one. If mimesis is a showing of the fact of telling, then Celie's letters are visual representations that attempt to tell the fact of showing. Whereas Hurston represents Janie's discovery of her voice as the enunciation of her own doubled self through a free indirect "narrative of division," Walker represents Celie's growth of self-consciousness as an act of writing. Janie and her narrator speak themselves into being; Celie, in her letters, writes herself into being. Walker Signifies upon Hurston by troping the concept of voice that unfolds in *Their Eyes Were Watching God*. Whereas Janie's movement from object to subject begins with her failure to recognize an image of her colored self in a photograph, precisely at a point in her childhood when she is known merely as "Alphabet" (a figure for all names and none), Celie's ultimate movement of self-negation is her self-description in her first letter to God: "I am." Celie, like Janie, is an absence, an erased presence, an empty set. Celie, moreover, writes in "Janie's voice," in a level of diction and within an idiom similar to that which Janie speaks. Celie, on the other hand, never speaks; rather, she writes her speaking voice and that of everyone who speaks to her.

This remarkably self-conscious Signifyin(g) strategy places *The Color Purple* in a direct line of descent from *Their Eyes Were Watching God*, in an act of literary bonding quite unlike anything that has ever happened within the Afro-American tradition. Walker, we well know, has written at length about her relationship to Zora Neale Hurston. I have always found it difficult to identify this bond textually, by which I mean that I have not found Hurston's presence in Walker's texts. In *The Color Purple*, however, Walker rewrites Hurston's narrative strategy, in an act of ancestral bonding that is especially rare in black letters, since, as we saw in Chapter 3, black writers have tended to trace their origins to white male parents.[7]

Walker, in effect, has written a letter of love to her authority figure, Hurston. While I am not aware of another epistolary novel in the Afro-American tradition, there is ample precedent in the tradition for the publication of letters. Ignatius Sancho's *Letters* were published at London in 1782. As we saw in Chapter 3, Phillis Wheatley's letters to Arbour Tanner were so well known by 1830 that they could be parodied in a broadside. Even the device of locating Celie's sister in Africa, writing letters home to her troubled sister, has a precedent in the tradition in Amanda Berry Smith's diarylike entries about her African missionary work, published in her *Autobiography* (1893).[8] But we do not have, before *The Color Purple*, an example of the epistolary novel in the black tradition of which I am aware

Why does Walker turn to the novel of letters to revise *Their Eyes Were Watching God?* As a way of concluding this study of voices in texts, and texts that somehow talk to other texts, I would like to discuss some of the implications of Walker's Signification upon Hurston's text by examining, if only briefly, a few of the more startling aspects of the rhetorical strategies at work in *The Color Purple* and its use of the epistolary form of narration.[9]

The Color Purple is comprised of letters written by two sisters, Celie and Nettie. Celie addresses her letters first to God and then to Nettie, while Nettie, off in the wilds of Africa as a missionary, writes her letters to Celie–letters intercepted by Celie's husband, stashed away in a trunk, and finally read by Celie and Shug Avery, her friend, companion, and lover. Nettie's unreceived letters to Celie appear, suddenly, almost at the center of the text (p. 107) and continue in what we might think of as the text's middle passage (to p. 150) with interruptions of three letters of Celie's addressed to God. Then Celie's addressee is Nettie, until she writes her final letter (pp. 242–44), which is addressed to God (twice) and to the stars, trees, the sky, to "peoples," and to "Everything." While I do not wish to diminish the importance of the novel's plot or its several echoes of moments in Hurston's novel, I am more interested here in suggesting the formal relationship that obtains between the strategies of narration of *Their Eyes* and of *The Color Purple*. Like Janie, Celie is married to a man who would imprison her, indeed brutalize her. Unlike Janie, however, Celie is liberated by her love for Shug Avery, the "bodaciously" strong singer with whom she shares the love that Janie shared with Tea Cake. It is Shug Avery, I shall argue, who stands in this text as Walker's figure for Hurston herself. Perhaps it will suffice to note that this is Celie's text, a text of becoming as is *Their Eyes*, but a becoming with a signal difference.

The most obvious difference between the two texts is that Celie writes herself into being, before our very eyes. Whereas Janie's moment of consciousness is figured as a ritual speech act, for Celie it is the written voice which is her vehicle for self-expression and self-revelation. We read the letters of the text, as it were, over Celie's shoulder, just as we overhear Janie telling her story to Phoeby as they sit on Janie's back porch. Whereas Janie and the narrator do most of Janie's speaking (in an idiomatic free indirect discourse), in *The Color Purple* two of the novel's three principal characters do all of the writing. Celie is her own author, in a manner that Janie could not possibly be, given the third-person form of narration of *Their Eyes*. To remind the reader that we are rereading letters, the lower border of each page of *The Color Purple* is demarcated by a solid black line, an imitation of how the border of a photoduplicated letter might look if bound in hardcover.

What is the text's motivation for the writing of letters? Nettie writes to Celie because she is far away in Africa. Celie writes to God for reasons that Nettie recapitulates in one of her letters:

> I remember one time you said your life made you feel so ashamed you couldn't even talk about it to God, you had to write it, bad as you thought your writing was. Well, now I know what you meant. And whether God will read letters or no, I know you will go on writing them; which is guidance enough for me. Anyway, when I don't write to you I feel as bad as I do when I don't pray, locked up in myself and choking on my own heart. I am so *lonely, Celie*. (p. 110)

The italicized command that opens the novel–"*You better not never tell nobody but God. It'd kill your mammy.*"–which we assume has been uttered by Celie's stepfather, is responded to literally by Celie. Celie writes to God for the same reason that Nettie writes to Celie, so that each may read the text of her life, almost exactly or simultaneously as events unfold.

This is the text's justification of its own representation of writing. But what are Walker's motivations? As I suggested above, Celie writes herself into being as a text, a text we are privileged to read over her shoulder. Whereas we are free to wonder aloud about the ironies of self-presentation in a double-voiced free indirect discourse, the epistolary strategy eliminates this aspect of reader response from the start. Celie writes her own story, and writes everyone else's tale in the text except Nettie's. Celie writes her text, and is a text, standing in discrete and episodic letters, which we, like voyeurs, hurriedly read before the addressees (God and Nettie) interrupt our stolen pleasures. Celie is a text in the same way in which Langston Hughes wrote (in *The Big Sea*) that Hurston was a book– "a perfect book of entertainment in herself."[10] We read Celie reading her world and writing it into being, in one subtle discursive act. There is no battle of voices here, as we saw in *Their Eyes*, between a disembodied narrator and a protagonist; Celie speaks–or writes–for Celie and, of course, to survive for Nettie, then for Shug, and finally for Celie.

Ironically, one of the well-known effects of the epistolary narrative is to underscore the illusion of the real, but also of the spontaneous.[11] The form allows for a maximum of identification with a character, precisely because the devices of empathy and distance, standard in third-person narration, no longer obtain. There is no apparent proprietary consciousness in the epistle, so readers must supply any coherence of interpretation of the text themselves. Samuel Richardson understood this well:

> It is impossible that readers the most attentive, can always enter
> into the views of the writer of a piece, written, as hoped, to
> Nature and the moment. A species of writing, too, that may be
> called new; and every one putting him and herself into the
> character they read, and judging of it by their own sensations.[12]

Celie recounts events, seemingly as they unfold; her readers decide their
meaning. Her readers piece together a text from the fragmented letters
which Celie never mails and which Celie, almost all at once, receives. But
Walker escapes the lack of control over how we read Celie precisely by
calling before us a writing style of such innocence with which only the most
hardened would not initially sympathize, then eventually *empathize*. By
showing Celie as the most utterly dynamic of characters, who comes to know
her world and to trust her readings of her world, and by enabling Celie to
compel from us compassion for the brutalities she is forced to suffer,
followed triumphantly by Celie's assertion of control (experiential control
that we learn of through her ever-increasing written control of her letters),
Walker manipulates our responses to Celie without even once revealing a
voice in the text that Celie or Nettie does not narrate or repeat or edit.

How is this different from first-person narrative in a fluid, or linear,
narrative? Again, a remarkably self-conscious Richardson tells us in *Clarissa*:

> Such a sweetness of temper, so much patience and resignation, as
> she seems to be mistress of; yet writing of and in the midst of
> *present* distresses! How *much more* lively and affecting, for that
> reason, must her style be; her mind tortured by the pangs of
> uncertainty (the events then hidden in the womb of fate) *than* the
> dry, narrative, unanimated style of persons, relating difficulties and
> dangers surmounted; the relator perfectly at ease; and if himself
> unmoved by his own story, not likely greatly to affect the reader![13]

Unlike the framed tales of Janie in *Their Eyes* or of the nameless
protagonist of *Invisible Man*, the reader of a novel of letters does not, indeed
cannot, know the outcome of Celie's tale until its writing ceases. The two
voices that narrate Ishmael Reed's "anti-detective" novel, for instance, are
troped in *The Color Purple* almost by a pun that turns upon this fact: whereas
a topos of *Mumbo Jumbo* is a supraforce searching for its text, for its
"writing," as Reed puts it, Celie emerges as a force, as a presence, by writing
all-too-short leters which, taken together, her readers weave or stitch
together as both the text of *The Color Purple* and the autobiographical text of
Celie's life and times, her bondage and her freedom. Celie charts her growth
of consciousness day to day, or letter to letter. By the end of the novel, we
know that Celie, like Reed's silent character, "jes' grew." Celie, moreover,
"jes' grew" by writing her text of herself. Whereas Reed's Jes Grew

disappears, at the end of *The Color Purple* we are holding Celie's text of herself in our hands. It is we who complete or close the circle or chain of Jes Grew Carriers, in an act of closure that Jes Grew's enemies disrupt in *Mumbo Jumbo*. When Nettie inevitably gets around to asking Celie how she managed to change so much, Celie quite probably could respond, "I jes' grew, I 'spose," precisely because the tyranny of the narrative present can only be overthrown by a linear reading of her letters, from first to last. Celie does not recapitulate her growth, as does Ellison's narrator or Hurston's Janie; only her readers have the leisure to reread Celie's text of development, the text of her becoming. Celie exists letter to letter; her readers supply the coherence necessary to speak of a precisely chartable growth, one measured by comparing or compiling all of the fragments of experience and feeling that Celie has selected to write.

Let us consider this matter of what I have called the tyranny of the narrative present. Celie, as narrator or author, presents herself to us, letter to letter, in a continuous written present. The time of writing is Celie's narrative present. We see this even more clearly when Celie introduces Nettie's first letter, the first letter that Celie and Shug recover from the attic trunk:

Dear God,
     This the letter I been holding in my hand. (p. 100)

The text of Nettie's letter follows, as an embedded narrative. This narrative present is comprised of (indeed, *can* be compromised of) only one event: the process of writing itself. All other events in *The Color Purple* are in the narrative past: no matter how near to the event Celie's account might be, the event is past, and it is this past about which Celie is writing.

We can see this clearly in Celie's first letter. The letter's first paragraph both underscores the moment of writing and provides a frame for the past events that Celie is about to share with her addressee, God:

Dear God,
     I am fourteen years old. I have always been a good girl.

Celie places her present self ("I am") under erasure, a device that reminds us that she is writing, and searching for her voice by selecting, then rejecting, word choice or word order, but also that there is some reason why Celie was once "a good girl" but no longer feels that she can make this claim before God. Because "a good girl" connotes the avoidance of sex, especially at the age of fourteen, we expect her fall from grace to be a fall of sensual pleasure. Celie tells us that we were right in this suspicion, but also wrong: there has been no pleasure involved in her "fall." Her account of the recent past explains:

Last spring after little Lucious come I heard them fussing. He was pulling on her arm. She say It too soon, Fonso, I ain't well. Finally he leave her alone. A week go by, he pulling on her arm again. she says Naw, I ain't gonna. Can't you see I'm already half dead, an all of these chilren.

She went to visit her sister doctor over Macon. Left me to see after the others. He never had a kine word to say to me. Just say You gonna do what your mammy wouldn't. First he put his thing up gainst my hip and sort of wiggle it around. Then he grab hold my titties. Then he push his thing inside my pussy. When that hurt, I cry. He start to choke me, saying You better shut up and git used to it.

But I don't never git used to it. And now I feels sick every time I be the one to cook. My mama she fuss at me an look at me. She happy, cause he good to her *now*. But too sick to last long. (p. 3; emphasis added)

Celie has been raped by the man she knows as her father. Her tale of woe has begun. Celie's first letter commences in a narrative present, shifts to a narrative past, then, in the letter's penultimate sentence, returns to a narrative present signified by "now." Prophetically, she even predicts the future, her mother's imminent death. In the narrative past, Celie develops, in fact controls, the representation of character and event. In the narrative present, Celie reveals to us that hers is the proprietary consciousness that we encounter in third-person narration, rendered in an epistle in a first-person narrative present. Celie, as author of her letters to God, might not be able to know what course events shall take, but the past belongs to her, salient detail by salient detail. We only know of Celie's life and times by her recounting of their significance and meaning, rendered in Celie's own word order. In this epistolary novel, the narrator of Celie's tale is identical with the author of Celie's letters. Because there is no gap here, as we saw in *Their Eyes* between the text's narrator and Janie, there would seem to be no need to bridge this gap through free indirect discourse.

This, however, is not the case in *The Color Purple*. While the gap between past and present is not obliterated, the gap between who sees and who speaks *is* obliterated by Celie's curious method of reporting discourse. The epistolary form's necessary shift between the narrative present and the narrative past creates the very space in which free indirect discourse dwells in Celie's narrative. It is in her representation of free indirect discourse that Walker undertakes her most remarkable revision of *Their Eyes Were Watching God*.

The Color Purple is replete with free indirect discourse. The double-voiced discourse of *Their Eyes* returns in the text of Celie's letters. Celie, as I have said, is the narrator and author of her letters. The narrator's voice, accordingly, is the voice of the protagonist. This protagonist, moreover, is divided into two parts: Celie, the character whose past actions we see represented in letters (an active but initially dominated and undereducated adolescent), and that other Celie, who–despite her use of written dialect–we soon understand is a remarkably reflective and sensitive teller, or writer, of a tale, or her own tale. Because of the curious interplay of the narrative past (in which Celie is a character) and a narrative present (in which Celie is the author), Celie emerges as both the subject and the object of narration. The subject-object split, or reconciliation, which we have seen in Hurston's use of free indirect discourse, in *The Color Purple* appears as the central rhetorical device by which Celie's self-consciousness is represented, in her own capacity to write a progressively better-structured story of herself.

Whereas Hurston represents Janie's emergent self in the shifting level of diction in the narrator's commentary and in the black-speech-informed indirect discourse, Walker represents Celie's dynamism in her ability to control her own narrative voice (that is, her own style of writing) but also in her remarkable ability to control all other voices spoken to Celie, which we encounter only in Celie's representation of them. Celie represents these voices, this spoken discourse, through the rhetorical device of free indirect discourse. It is Celie's voice that is always a presence whenever anyone in her world is represented as having spoken. We can, therefore, never be certain whether a would-be report, or mimesis, of dialogue is Celie's or the character's whose words we are overhearing or, more precisely, reading over Celie's shoulder.

Let me be clear: no one speaks in this novel. Rather, two sisters correspond to each other, through letters which one never receives (Celie's) and which the other receives almost all at once (Nettie's). There is no true mimesis, then, in *The Color Purple*, only diegesis. But, through Celie's mode of apparently reporting speech, underscored dramatically by her written dialect voice of narration, we logically assume that we are being shown discourse, when all along we never actually are. Celie only tells us what people have said to her. She never shows us their words in direct quotation. Precisely because her written dialect voice is identical in diction and idiom to the supposedly spoken words that pepper her letters, we believe that we are overhearing people speak, just as Celie did when the words were in fact uttered. We are not, however; indeed, we can never be certain whether or not Celie is showing us a telling or telling us a showing, as awkward as this sounds. In the speeches of her characters, Celie's voice and a character's merge into one, almost exactly as we saw happen in *Their Eyes* when Janie and her narrator speak in the merged voice of free indirect discourse. In these passages from *The Color Purple*, the distinction between mimesis and diegesis is apparently obliterated: the opposition between them has collapsed.

This innovation, it seems to me, is Walker's most brilliant stroke, her most telling Signifyin(g) move on Hurston's text. Let us examine just a few of scores of examples. The first is Celie's account of Mr. —'s sisters, named Carrie and Kate, as one of Walker's Signifyin(g) gestures toward Jean Toomer's *Cane*, where Carrie Kate appears as a central character in "Kabnis."[14] (Walker, incidentally, loves *Cane* almost as much as she does *Their Eyes*, as she writes in "Zora Neale Hurston: A Cautionary Tale and a Partisan View."[15]) Celie's depiction of Carrie and Kate's discourse follows:

> Well that's no excuse, say the first one, Her name Carrie, other one name Kate. When a woman marry she spose to keep a decent house and a clean family. Why, wasn't nothing to come here in the winter time and all these children have colds, they have flue, they have direar, they have newmonya, they have worms, they have the chill and fever. They hungry. They hair ain't comb. They too nasty to touch. (p. 19)

Who is speaking in these passages: Carrie and Kate, or Celie, or all three? All three are speaking, or, more properly, no one is speaking, because Celie has merged whatever was actually said with her own voice and has written it out for us in a narrative form that aspires to the spoken but never represents or reports anyone else's speech but Celie's on one hand, and Celie-cum-characters' on the other. Celie is in control of her narration, even to the point of controlling everyone else's speech, which her readers cannot encounter without hearing their words merged with Celie's.

We can see Celie's free indirect discourse in another example, which reveals how sophisticated an editor Celie becomes, precisely as she grows in self-awareness.[16] Celie is introducing, or framing, one of Nettie's letters, in a narrative present:

> It's hot, here, Celie, she write. Hotter than July. Hotter than August *and* July. Hot like cooking dinner on a big stove in a little kitchen in August and July. Hot. (p. 126)

Who said, or wrote, these words, words which echo both the Southern expression "a cold day in August" and Stevie Wonder's album *Hotter Than July?* Stevie Wonder? Nettie? Celie? All three, and no one. These are Celie's words, merged with Nettie's, in a written imitation of the merged voices of free indirect discourse, an exceptionally rare form in that here even the illusion of mimesis is dispelled.

I could cite several more examples, but one more shall suffice. This moving scene appears just as Celie and Shug are beginning to cement their bond, a bond that bespeaks a sisterly, and later a sexual, bonding:

Shug saying Celie. Miss Celie. And I look up where she at.

She say my name again. She say this song I'm bout to sing is call Miss Celie's song. Cause she scratched it out of my head when I was sick. . . .

First time somebody made something and name it after me.

(p. 65)

Once again, Celie's voice and Shug's are merged together into one, one we think is Shug's but which can only be Celie's-and-Shug's, simultaneous, inseparable, bonded.

What are we to make of Walker's remarkable innovation in Hurston's free indirect discourse? We can assume safely that one of Hurston's purposes in the narrative strategies at play in *Their Eyes* was to show James Weldon Johnson and Countee Cullen, and just about everyone else in the New Negro Renaissance that dialect not only was not limited to two stops–humor and pathos–but was fully capable of being used as a literary language even to write a novel. Dialect, black English vernacular and its idiom, as a literary device was not merely a figure of spoken speech; rather, for Hurston, it was a storehouse of figures. As if in a coda to the writing of *Their Eyes*, Hurston even published a short story entirely in the vernacular, entitled "Story in Harlem Slang" (1942), complete with a "Glossary."[17] Yet, just as Johnson had edited or interpreted the language of the black vernacular in his rendition of the "Seven Sermons in Verse" that comprise *God's Trombones* (1927), so too had Hurston merged dialect and standard English in the idiom of the free indirect discourse that gradually overtakes the narrative commentary in *Their Eyes*. Hurston showed the tradition just how dialect could blend with standard English to create a new voice, a voice exactly as black as it is white. (Johnson, of course, had "translated" from the vernacular into standard English.) Walker's Signifyin(g) riff on Hurston was to seize upon the device of free indirect discourse as practiced in *Their Eyes* but to avoid standard English almost totally in Celie's narration. Walker has written a novel in dialect, in the black vernacular. The initial impression that we have of Celie's naiveté slowly reveals how one can write an entire novel in dialect. This, we must realize, is as important a troping of *Their Eyes* as is the page-by-page representation of Celie's writing of her own tale. If Hurston's writing aspired to the speakerly, then Walker's apparently speaking characters turn out to have been written.

There are other parallels between the two texts which provide evidence of their Signifyin(g) relationship. Whereas Janie's sign of self-awareness is represented as her ability to tell Phoeby her own version of events, Walker matches this gesture by having Celie first write her own texts, discover her sister's purloined letters, arrange them with Shug in "some kind of order," as

Shug says to Celie, then read them so that a second narrative unfolds which both completes and implicitly comments on Celie's narrative which has preceded it by 106 of the text's pages. This newly recovered narrative is a parallel text. This initial cache of unreceived letters functions as a framed tale within Celie's tale, as do Nettie's subsequently received letters, recapitulating events and providing key details absent from Celie's story. Nettie's letters are written in standard English, not only to contrast her character to Celie's but also to provide some relief from Celie's language. But even this narrative Celie controls, by ordering their reading but especially by introducing them, within her letters, with her own commentary. Nettie's letters function as a second narrative of the past, echoing the shift from present to past that we see within the time shifts of Celie's letters. But Nettie's discovered letters are *The Color Purple*'s structural revision of Janie's bracketed tale. We recognize a new Celie once Nettie's letters have been read. Celie's last letter to God reads:

Dear God,

That's it, say Shug. Pack your stuff. You coming back to Tennessee with me.

But I feels daze.

My daddy lynch. My mama crazy. All my little half-brothers and sisters no kin to me. My children not my sister and brother. Pa not pa.

You must be sleep. (p. 151)

Order has been restored, the incest taboo has not been violated, Celie is confused but free and moving.

Janie's Signifyin(g) declaration of independence read in the starkest of terms to her husband, Joe, in *Their Eyes* is repeated in *The Color Purple*. As Celie is about to leave with Shug, this exchange occurs between her and her husband:

Celie is coming with us, say Shug.

Mr. _____'s head swivel back straight. Say what? he ast.

Celie is coming to Memphis with me.

Over my dead body, Mr. _____ say,

. . . what wrong now?

You a lowdown dog is what's wrong, I say. It's time to leave you and enter into the Creation. And your dead body just the welcome mat I need.

Say what? he ast. Shock.

All round the table folkses mouths be dropping open. . . .

Mr. _____ start to sputter. ButButButButBut. Sound like some kind of motor. (p. 170)

This marvelous exchange refigures that between Janie and Joe. Celie's newly found voice makes "folkses mouths" drop open, and Mr. ——'s voice inarticulate and dehumanized, "like some kind of motor." A bit later, Celie continues, in triumph, to curse her oppressor:

> Any more letters come? I ast.
> He say, What?
> You heard me, I say. Any more letters from Nettie come?
> If they did, he say, I wouldn't give 'em to you. You two of a kind, he say. A man try to be nice to you, you fly in his face.
> I curse you, I say.
> What that mean? he say.
> I say, Until you do right by me, everything you touch will crumble. (pp. 175–76)

This quasi-Hoodoo curse reads like one of Hurston's recipes for revenge that she published in her classic work on Vaudou, entitled *Tell My Horse* (1938). Significantly, these exchanges–Celie's first open defiance of her husband, Albert–are repeated or written in Celie's first two letters addressed to Nettie rather than to God. Celie's husband's desparate response follows:

> He laugh. Who you think you is? he say. You can't curse nobody. Look at you. You black, you pore, you ugly, you a woman. Goddam, he say, you nothing at all. (p. 176)

But Albert no longer has the power of the word over Celie, just as in Hurston Joe cannot recoup from Janie's Signifyin(g) on his manhood in public. This exchange continues:

> Until you do right by me, I say, everything you even dream about will fail. I give it to him straight, just like it come to me. And it seem to come to me from the trees.
> Whoever heard of such a thing, say Mr. ——. I probably didn't whup your ass enough.
> Every lick you hit me you will suffer twice, I say. Then I say, You better stop talking because all I'm telling you ain't coming just from me. Look like when I open my mouth the air rush in and shape words.
> Shit, he say. I should have lock you up. Just let you out to work.
> The jail you plan for me is the one in which you will rot, I say....
> I'll fix her wagon! say Mr. ——, and spring toward me.
> A dust devil flew up on the porch between us, fill my mouth with dirt. The dirt say, Anything you do to me, already done to you.

Then I feel Shug shake me. Celie, she say. And I come to myself.

I'm pore, I'm black, I may be ugly and can't cook, a voice say to everything listening. But I'm here.

Amen, say Shug. Amen, amen. (p. 176)

Celie has at last issued her liberating (and liberated) call, while her friend Shug, like any black audience, provides the proper ritual response to a masterful performance: "Amen, say Shug. Amen, amen." Celie speaks herself free, as did Janie, but in a speaking we know only by its writing, in a letter to Nettie. Celie has conquered her foe, Albert, and the silences in her self, by representing an act of speech in the written word, in which she turns Albert's harsh curses back on him, masterfully.

Just as this scene of instruction echoes Janie's, so too is *The Color Purple* full of other thematic echoes of *Their Eyes Were Watching God*. Houses confine in *The Color Purple* just as they do in *Their Eyes*, but Celie, Nettie, Shug, and Janie all find a form of freedom in houses in which there are no men: Nettie's hut in Africa, Shug's mansion in Tennessee, and Janie's empty home in Eatonville. The home that Nettie and Celie inherit will include men, but men respectful of the inherent strength and equality of women. Celie and Nettie own this home, and the possession of property seems to preclude the domination of men.

Shug would seem to be a refugee from *Their Eyes*. It is Shug who teaches Celie that God is not an "old white man," that God is nature and love and even sex, that God is a sublime feeling:

Here's the thing, say Shug. The thing I believe. God is inside you and inside everybody else. You come into the world with God. But only them that search for it inside find it. And sometimes it just manifest itself even if you not looking, or don't know what you looking for. Trouble do it for most folks, I think. Sorrow, lord. Feeling like shit.

It? I ast.

Yeah, It. God ain't a he or a she, but a It.

But what do it look like? I ast.

Don't look like nothing, she say. It ain't a picture show. It ain't something you can look at apart from anything else, including yourself. I believe God is everything, say Shug. Everything that is or ever was or ever will be. And when you can feel that, and be happy to feel that, you've found It. (pp. 166–67)

But it is also Shug who teaches Celie about Janie's lyrical language of the trees, a language of nature in which God speaks in the same metaphors in which he spoke to Janie, a divine utterance which led Janie to enjoy her first orgasm, an experience that Shug tells Celie is God's ultimate sign of presence:

> She say, My first step from the old white man was trees. Then air. Then birds. Then other people. But one day when I was sitting quiet and feeling like a motherless child, which I was, it come to me: that feeling of being part of everything, not separate at all. I knew that if I cut a tree, my arm would bleed. And I laughed and I cried and I run all round the house. I knew just what it was. In fact, when it happen, you can't miss it. It sort of like you know what, she say, grinning and rubbing high up on my thigh.
>
> *Shug!* I say.
>
> Oh, she say. God love all them feelings. That's some of the best stuff
>
> God did. And when you know God loves 'em you enjoys 'em a lot more. You can just relax, go with everything that's going, and praise God by liking what you like.
>
> God don't think it dirty? I ast. (p. 167)

God don't think it dirty? I ast. (p. 167) And if we miss Shug's connection with Janie, Walker first describes Shug in terms in which she has described Hurston:

> She do more then that. She git a picture. The first one of a real person I ever seen. She say Mr.—was taking something out his billfold to show Pa an it fell out an slid under the table. Shug Avery was a woman. The most beautiful woman I ever saw. She more pretty then my mama. She bout ten thousand times more prettier then me. I see her there in furs. Her face rouge. Her hair like somethin tail. She grinning with her foot up on somebody motocar. Her eyes serious tho. Sad some. (p. 8)

Compare that description with Walker's description of Hurston:

> [She] loved to wear hats, tilted over one eye, and pants and boots. (I have a photograph of [Hurston] in pants, boots, and broadbrim that was given to me by her brother, Everette. She has her foot up on the running board of a car–presumably hers, and bright red–and looks racy.)[18]

There are several other echoes, to which I shall allude only briefly. Celie's voice, when she first speaks out against the will of Mr. ——, "seem to come to me from the trees" (p. 176) just as Janie's inner voice manifests itself under the pear tree. Celie, like Janie, describes herself as a "motherless child" (p. 167). Key metaphors repeat: Hurston's figure of nature mirroring Janie's emotions–"the rose of the world was breathing out smell" (*Their Eyes*, p. 23)–becomes Shug and Celie's scene in which Shug teaches Celie to masturbate, using a mirror to watch herself:

> I stand there with the mirror.
>
> She say, What, too shame even to go off and look at yourself? And you look so cute too, she say, laughing. All dressed up for Harpo's, smelling good and everything, but scared to look at your own pussy. . . .
>
> I lie back on the bed and haul up my dress. Yank down my bloomers. Stick the looking glass tween my legs. Ugh. All that hair. Then my pussy lips be black. Then inside look like a wet rose.
>
> It a lot prettier than you thought, ain't it? she say from the door. (p. 69)

Later, in her first letter to Nettie, Celie uses the figure of the rose again in a simile: "Shug a beautiful something, let me tell you. She frown a little, look out cross the yard, lean back in her chair, look like a big rose" (p. 167).

In the same way that Walker's extends to the literal Hurston's figure of the rose of the world breathing out smell, she also erases the figurative aspect of Janie's metaphor for her narration to Phoeby ("mah tongue is in mah friend's mouf") by making Shug and Celie literal "kissin-friends," or lovers. That which is implicit in Hurston's figures Walker makes explicit. Walker, in addition, often reverses Hurston's tropes: whereas *Their Eyes* accounts for the orgasm Janie experiences under the pear tree by saying, in free indirect discourse, "So this was a marriage!" (p. 24), Celie writes that when Mr. _____ beats her, she turns herself into a tree:

> He beat me like he beat the children. Cept he don't never hardly beat them. He say, Celie, git the belt. The children be outside the room peeking through the cracks. It all I can do not to cry. I make myself wood. I say to myself, Celie, you a tree. That's how come I know trees fear man. (p. 22)

Their Eyes' circular narration, in which the end is the beginning and the beginning the end, *The Color Purple* tropes with a linear narration. There are several other examples of these Signifyin(g) riffs.

Walker has Signified upon Hurston in what must stand to be the most loving revision, and claim to title, that we have seen in the tradition. Walker has turned to a black antecedent text to claim literary ancestry, or motherhood, not only for content but for structure. Walker's turn to Hurston for form (and to, of all things, the topoi of medieval romance known as "The Incestuous Father" and "The Exchanged Letter" for plot structure),[19] openly disrupts the patterns of revision (white form, black content) that we have discussed in Chapter 3. Even Walker's representation of Celie's writing in dialect echoes Hurston's definition of an "oral hieroglyphic," and her ironic use of speakerly language which no person can ever speak, because it exists only in a written text. This, too, Walker tropes, by a trick of figuration, one so clever that only Esu's female principle could have inspired it: people who speak dialect *think* that they are saying standard English words; when they write the words that they speak as "dis" or "dat," therefore, they spell "this" and "that." Walker, like Hurston, masters the illusion of the black vernacular by its writing, in a masterful exemplification of the black trope of Stylin' out.

Walker's revision of Hurston stands at the end of a chain of narration. Walker's text, like those by Toni Morrison, James Baldwin, Ann Petry, Paule Marshall, Leon Forrest, Ernest Gaines, John Wideman, and others, afford subsequent writers tropes and topoi to be revised. Endings, then, imply beginnings. Increasingly, however, after Walker and Reed, black authors could even more explicitly turn to black antecedent texts for both form and content. The tradition of Afro-American literature, a tradition of grounded repetition and difference, is characterized by its urge to start over, to begin again, but always to begin on a well-structured foundation. Our narrators, our Signifiers, are links in an extended ebony chain of discourse, which we, as critics, protect and explicate. As Martin Buber puts the relation in *The Legend of Baal-Shem*:

> I have told it anew as one who was born later. I bear in me the blood and spirit of those who created it, and out of my blood and spirit it has become new. I stand in the chain of narrators, a link between links; I tell once again the old stories, and if they sound new it is because the new already lay dormant in them when they were told for the first time.

While the principal silent second text is *Their Eyes Were Watching God*, Walker's critique of Celie's initial conception of God, and especially its anthropomorphism, revises a key figure in Rebecca Cox Jackson's narrative and perhaps surfaces as a parable for the so-called noncanonical critic.

Just after Celie and Shug have discovered, arranged, and read Nettie's purloined letters, Celie writes this to Nettie:

Dear Nettie,
> I don't write to God no more, I write to you.
> What happen to God? as Shug.
> Who that? I say.
> . . . what God do for me? I ast.
> She say, Celie! Like she shock. He gave you life, good health,
and a good woman that love you to death.

Yeah, I say, and he give me a lynched daddy, a crazy mama, a lowdown dog of a step pa and a sister I probably won't ever see again. Anyhow, I say, the God I been praying and writing to is a man. And act just like all the other mens I know. Trifling, forgitful, and lowdown. (p. 164)

A few pages later, Shug describes to Celie the necessity of escaping the boundaries caused by the anthropomorphism of God and calls this concept that of "the old white man" (p. 167). This, Celie confesses, is difficult: "Well, us talk and talk bout God, but I'm still adrift. Trying to chase that old white man out of my head" (p. 168). Shug responds that the problem is not only "the old white man," but all men:

Still, it is like Shug say, You have go to git man off your eyeball, before you can see anything a'tall.

Man corrup everything, say Shug. He on your box of grits, in your hand, and all over the road. He try to make you think he everywhere. Soon as you think he everywhere, you think he God. But he ain't. Whenever you trying to pray, and man plop himself on the other end of it, tell him to git lost, say Shug. Conjure up flowers, wind, water, a big rock. (p. 168)

This passage, most certainly, constitutes an important feminist critique of the complex fiction of male domination. But it also recalls a curious scene in Rebecca Cox Jackson's text. Indeed, Walker's text Signifies upon it. Earlier, I discussed Jackson's supernatural mastery of literacy. Jackson was careful to show that God's gracious act of instruction freed her from the domination and determination of her words (their order, their meaning) by her minister-brother, who by rearranging her words sought to control their sense. Jackson indeed became free, and freely interprets the Word of God in her own, often idiosyncratic way. But is Jackson's a truly liberating gesture, a fundamental gesture of a nascent feminism?

Jackson substitutes a mystical "white man," the image of whom Shug and Celie seek to dispel, for the interpretive role of the male, the relation of truth to understanding, of sound and sense. Jackson's account is strikingly vivid:

A white man took me by my right hand and led me on the north side of the room, where sat a square table. On it lay a book open. And he said to me, "Thou shall be instructed in this book, from Genesis to Revelations." And then he took me on the west side, where stood a table. And it looked like the first. And said, "Yea, thou shall be instructed from the beginning of creation to the end of time." And then he took me on the east side of the room also, where stood a table and book like the two first, and said, "I will instruct thee–yea, thou shall be instructed from the beginning of all things to the end of all things. Yea, thou shall be well instructed. I will instruct."

When Samuel handed me to this man at my own back door, he turned away. I never saw him any more. When this man took me by the hand, his hand was soft like down. He was dressed all in light drab. He was bareheaded. His countenance was serene and solemn and divine. There was a father and a brother's countenance to be seen in his face.

And then I awoke, and I saw him as plain as I did in my dream. And after that he taught me daily. And when I would be reading and come to a hard word, I would see him standing by my side and he would teach me the word right. And often, when I would be in meditation and looking into things which was hard to understand, I would find him by me, teaching and giving me understanding. And oh, his labor and care which he had with me often caused me to weep bitterly, when I would see my great ignorance and the great trouble he had to make me understand eternal things. For I was so buried in the depth of the tradition of my forefathers, that it did seem as if I never could be dug up.[20]

Jackson opposes the "white man" who would "teach me the word right," he who would stand "by me, teaching and giving me understanding," with the delineation of understanding imposed by her brother and, curiously enough, by "the depth of the tradition of my forefathers." So oppressive was the latter that, she admits, "it did seem as if I never could be dug up."

Shug and Celie's conception of God Signifies upon these passages from Jackson. Jackson's "white man" and Celie's, the speaking interpreter and the silent reader, are identical until Celie, with Shug's help, manages to "git man off your eyeball." Whereas Jackson suffocates under the burden of tradition, "buried in the depth" as she puts it, Walker's text points to a bold new model for a self-defined, or internally defined, notion of tradition, one black and female. The first step toward such an end, she tells us, was to eliminate the "white man" to whom we turn for "teaching" and the "giving [of] understanding." This parable of interpretation is Walker's boldest claim about the nature and function of the black tradition and its interpretation. To turn away from, to step outside the white hermeneutical circle and into the black is the challenge issued by Walker's critique of Jackson's vision.

NOTES

1. Rebecca Cox Jackson, *Gifts of Power: The Writings of Rebecca Jackson, Black Visionary, Shaker Eldress*, ed. by Jean McMahon Humez (Amherst: University of Massachusetts Press, 1981). See Alice Walker, "Gifts of Power: The Writings of Rebecca Jackson," in *In Search of Our Mothers' Gardens: Womanist Prose by Alice Walker* (New York: Harcourt Brace Jovanovich, 1983), pp. 71–82. The review first appeared in the November–December 1981 issue of *Black Scholar*. In a letter, Walker has informed me that Jackson's book "was the first book I read (I read almost nothing while writing *The Color Purple*) and reviewed *after* I finished. I took it as a sign that I was on the right track." The uncanny resemblances between key figures in Jackson's and Walker's texts suggest that forms of tradition and patterns of revision can be remarkably complex, indeed cultural.

2. Jackson, *Gifts of Power*, p. 107.

3. Ibid.

4. Ibid., pp. 107–8.

5. Ibid., p. 108.

6. Walker, "Gifts of Power," p. 73.

7. For Walker's explicit comments on Hurston, see *In Search of Our Mothers' Gardens*, pp. 83–116.

8. Amanda Smith, *An Autobiography: The Story of the Lord's Dealings with Mrs. Amanda Smith, the Colored Evangelist; Containing an Account of her Life Work of Faith, and her Travels in America, England, Ireland, Scotland, India and Africa, as an Independent Missionary* (1893; Chicago: Christian Witness Co., 1921). I wish to thank Mary Helen Washington for pointing this out to me.

9. Alice Walker, *The Color Purple* (New York: Harcourt Brace Jovanovich, 1982).

10. Quoted in Walker, *In Search of Our Mothers' Gardens, p. 100.*

11. Terry Eagleton discusses these aspects of epistolary fiction in *The rape of Clarissa: Writing, Sexuality and Class Struggle in Samuel Richardson* (Minneapolis: University of Minnesota Press, 1982), p. 25.

12. Cited in ibid., p. 25.

13. Ibid., p. 26.

14. Jean Toomer, *cane*, p. 204. Walker informs me that "All names in *Purple* are *family* or Eatonton, Georgia, community names. Kate was my father's mother. In real life she was the model for Annie Julia (in the novel), my grandfather's 'illegitimate' daughter (who in the novel is the wife, but who in real life was the granddaughter of Albert who in the novel is her father). It was *she*, Kate, my grandmother, who was murdered by her lover (he shot her) when my dad was eleven. Carrie was an aunt. But your version is nice, too, and my version is so confusing. For instance, the germ for Celie is Rachel, my step-grandmother: she of the poem 'Burial' in *Revolutionary Petunias*."

15. Walker writes, "*There is no book more important to me than this one* (including Toomer's *Cane*, which comes close, but from what I recognize is a more perilous direction)." *In Search of Our Mothers' Gardens*, p. 86. See also "The Divided Life of Jean Toomer," pp. 60–65.

16. Kate Nickerson points this out in an unpublished essay, "'From Listening to the Rest': On Literary Discourse Between Zora Neale Hurston and Alice Walker," p. 57.

17. Zora Neale Hurston, "Story in Harlem Slang," *The American Mercury* 45 (July 1942): 84–96.

18. Walker, "Zora Neale Hurston," p. 88.

19. See Margaret Schlauch, *Chaucer's Constance and Accused Queens* (New York: New York University Press, 1927), pp. 63–69. I am deeply appreciative of Dr. Elizabeth Archibald for pointing this out to me.

20. Jackson, *Gifts of Power*, pp. 146–47.

Chronology

1944   Birth of Alice Walker (February 9)

1952   Loses sight in one eye when her brother accidentally shoots her with a BB gun

1958   Surgery removes large cataract from blind eye, restoring the eye aesthetically

1961   Enters Spelman College in Atlanta, Georgia

1963   Transfers to Sarah Lawrence College in Bronxville, New York

1964   Undergoes an illegal abortion in the fall; becomes suicidal; begins to write

1965   Receives degree from Sarah Lawrence College; moves back to Georgia, where she registers voters door to door; moves to New York City in the autumn and works for the Welfare Department

1966   Awarded fellowship from Bread Loaf Writer's Conference; moves to Mississippi; meets Melvyn Leventhal; the couple return to New York City for his final year of law school; wins the *American Scholar* essay contest

1967   Short story "To Hell with Dying" appears in anthology; marries Leventhal (March 17); Walker and Leventhal move to Mississippi; works for Head Start

1968   Miscarries, one week after the funeral of Dr. Martin Luther King Jr.; *Once: Poems* is published

1969   Birth of Rebecca Walker (November 17)

1970   *The Third Life of Grange Copeland* is published

1972   Accepts temporary teaching positions at Wellesley College and the University of Massachusetts

1973   *Revolutionary Petunias and Other Poems* and *In Love and Trouble: Stories of Black Women* are published; death of Willie Lee Walker

1974   Returns with Leventhal and Rebecca Walker to New York City; *Langston Hughes: An American Poet*, a children's book, is published

1976   Divorce from Leventhal; *Meridian* is published

1978   Moves to San Francisco

1979   *Goodnight, Willie Lee, I'll See You in the Morning* is published; with Robert Allen, moves to home in Mendocino, California

1981   *You Can't Keep a Good Woman Down* is published

1982   *The Color Purple* is published

1983   Wins both the American Book Award and the Pulitzer Prize for *Purple*; *In Search of Our Mothers' Gardens: Womanist Prose* is published; onset of symptoms of Lyme disease

1984   Writes screenplay for *The Color Purple*; with Robert Allen, founds Wild Trees Press; *Horses Make a Landscape Look More Beautiful* is published

1985   Spends summer on the set of film *The Color Purple*, which is released that December

1986   Film *Purple* receives 11 Academy Award nominations but wins no Oscars

1988   *To Hell with Dying*, illustrated children's book; closing of Wild Trees Press; *Living by the Word: Selected Writings 1973–1986* is published

1989   *The Temple of My Familiar* is published

1991   *Her Blue Body Everything We Know: Earthling Poems 1965–1990 Complete* and *Finding the Green Stone*, a children's book, are published

1992   *Possessing the Secret of Joy* is published; film and book titled *Warrior Marks: Female Genital Mutilation and the Sexual Blinding of Women* are released

1993   Death of Minnie Tallulah Grant Walker (September)

1996   *The Same River Twice: Honoring the Difficult* is published

1997   *Anything We Love Can Be Saved: A Writer's Activism* is published

1998   *By the Light of My Father's Smile* is published

1999   Is featured in PBS documentary "I'll Make Me a World: A Century of African-American Arts"

2000   *The Way Forward Is with a Broken Heart* is released

2001   *Sent by Earth: A Message from the Grandmother Spirit After the Bombing of the World Trade Center and the Pentagon* (December 27)

Works by Alice Walker

FICTION

The Third Life of Grange Copeland. 1970
In Love and Trouble: Stories of Black Women. 1973
Meridian. 1976
You Can't Keep a Good Woman Down. 1981
The Color Purple. 1982
The Temple of My Familiar. 1989
Possessing the Secret of Joy. 1992
By the Light of My Father's Smile. 1998
The Way Forward Is with a Broken Heart. 2000

NONFICTION

In Search of Our Mothers' Gardens: Womanist Prose. 1983
Living by the Word: Selected Writings 1973-1987. 1988
Warrior Marks: Female Genital Mutilation and the Sexual Blinding of Women.
    1992
The Same River Twice: Honoring the Difficult. 1996
Anything We Love Can Be Saved: A Writer's Activism. 1997
Sent by Earth: A Message from the Grandmother Spirit After the Bombing of the
    World Trade Center and the Pentagon. December 2001

POETRY

Once: Poems. 1968
Revolutionary Petunias and Other Poems. 1973
Goodnight, Willie Lee, I'll See You in the Morning. 1979
Horses Make a Landscape Look More Beautiful. 1986
Her Blue Body Everything We Know: Earthling Poems 1965–1990 Complete. 1991

CHILDREN'S BOOKS

Langston Hughes: An American Poet. 1974
To Hell with Dying. 1988
Finding the Green Stone. 1991

Works about Alice Walker

Abbandonato, Linda. "A View from 'Elsewhere': Subversive Sexuality and the Rewriting of the Heroine's Story in *The Color Purple*." *PMLA* 6 (Oct 1991): 1106–1115.

———. *Womanist & Feminist Aesthetics: A Comparative Review*. Athens, Ohio: Ohio University Press, 1995.

———. "Womanism Revisited: Women and the (Ab)use of Power in *The Color Purple*." In *Feminist Nightmares: Women at Odds. Feminism and the Problem of Sisterhood*, edited by Susan Ostrov Weisser and Jennifer Fleischner, 88–105. New York and London: New York University Press, 1994.

Awkward, Michael. *Inspiring Influences: Tradition, Revision and Afro-American Women's Novels*. New York: Columbia University Press, 1991.

Babb, Valerie. "*The Color Purple*: Writing to Undo What Writing Has Done." *Phylon* 47 (June 1986): 107–16.

Baker, Jr., Houston A. and Charlotte Pierce-Baker. "Patches: Quilts and Community in Alice Walker's 'Everyday Use.'" In *Alice Walker: "Everyday Use,"* edited by Barbara Christian, 149–165. Women Writers: Texts and Contexts. New Bruswick, New Jersey: Rutgers University Press, 1994.

Banks, Erma Davis, and Keith Byerman. *Alice Walker: An Annotated Bibliography, 1968-1986*. New York & London: Garland Publishing, Inc., 1989.

Bauer, Margaret D. "Alice Walker: Another Southern Writer Criticizing Codes Not Put To 'Everyday Use.'" *Studies in Short Fiction* 29 (Spring 1992): 143–51.

Bell, Roseann P., Bettye J. Parker, and Beverly Guy-Sheftall, eds. *Sturdy Black Bridges: Visions of Black Women in Literature*. Garden City, New York: Anchor-Doubleday, 1979.

Bernstein, Richard. "New Age Anthropology in Old Mexico." *New York Times*, 7 October 1998.

Bloom, Harold, ed. *Alice Walker*. Modern Critical Views. New York: Chelsea House Publishers, 1989.

————, ed. *Alice Walker's The Color Purple*. Modern Critical Interpretations. Philadelphia: Chelsea House Publishers, 2000.

Bobo, Jacqueline. "Shifting through the Controversy: Reading *The Color Purple*." *Callaloo: An Afro-American and African Journal of Arts and Letters* 2, no. 2 (Spring 1989): 332–42.

Brock, Sabine and Anne Koenen. "Alice Walker in Search of Zora Neale Hurston: Rediscovering a Black Female Tradition." In *History and Tradition in Afro-American Culture*, edited by Gunter H. Leenz. Frankfurt: Campus, 1984.

Broussard, Sharon. "Male-Bashing Dominates Walker's Latest Effort." *Cleveland Plain Dealer*, 18 October 1998.

Bun, Austin. "Walker, in Her Own Shoes." *Advocate*, 27 February 2001.

Butler, Cheryl B. "The Color Purple Controversy: Black Women Spectatorship." *Wide Angle: A Film Quarterly of Theory, Criticism, and Practice* 3, no. 3–4 (1991): 62–69.

Butler, Robert James. "Alice Walker's Vision of the South in *The Third Life of Grange Copeland*." *African American Review* 27, no. 2 (Summer 1993): 195–204.

Butler-Evans, Elliot. *Race, Gender, and Desire: Narrative Strategies in the Fiction of Toni Cade Bambara, Toni Morrison, and Alice Walker*. Philadelphia: Temple University Press, 1989.

Byerman, Keith. "Desire and Alice Walker: The Quest for a Womanist Narrative." *Callaloo* 12 (Spring 1989): 343-45.

————. "Gender and Justice: Alice Walker and the Sexual Politics of Civil Rights." In *The World is Our Home: Society and Culture in Contemporary Southern Writing*, edited by Jeffrey J. Folks and Nancy Summer Folks, 93-106. Lexington: University Press of Kentucky, 2000.

Chambers, Kimberly. "Right on Time: History and Religion in Alice Walker's *The Color Purple*." *CLA Journal* 31 (September 1987): 44–62.

Cheung, King-Kok. "'Don't Tell': Imposed Silences in *The Color Purple* and in *The Woman Warrior*." *PMLA* 103 (March 1988): 162–74.

Christian, Barbara. "The Contrary Black Women Of Alice Walker." *Black Scholar* 12 (March–April 1981): 21—30, 70–71.

————. "No More Buried Loves: The Themes of Lesbianism in Lorde, Naylor, Shange, Walker." *Feminist Issues* 5, no. 1 (Spring 1985): 3–20.

————. "Novels for Everyday Use: The Novels of Alice Walker." In *Black Women Novelists*, 180–238. Westport, Connecticut: Greenwood, 1980.

Davenport, Doris. "Afracentric Visions." *The Women's Review of Books* 6, no. 20 (September 1989): 13–14.

Davis, Thadious. "Alice Walker's Celebration of Self in Southern Generations." In *Women Writers of the Contemporary South*, edited by Peggy Whitman Prenshaw, 39–53. Jackson: University Press of Mississippi, 1984.

————. "Poetry as Preface to Fiction." In *Alice Walker: Critical Perspectives Past and Present*, edited by Henry Louis Gates, Jr. and K. A. Appiah, 275–283. New York: Amistad Press, 1993.

Demby, David. "Purple People-Eater." *New Yorker*, 13 Jan.1986, 56.

Dieke, Ikenna. "Introduction: Alice Walker, A Woman Walking into Peril." In *Critical Essays on Alice Walker*, edited by Ikenna Dieke, 1–12. Contributions in Afro-American and African Studies, no. 189. Westport, Connecticut & London: Greenwood Press, 1999.

DuPlessis, Rachel Blau. *Writing Beyond the Ending: Narrative Strategies of Twentieth-Century Women Writers*. Bloomington: Indian University Press, 1985.

Early, Gerald. "*The Color Purple* as Everybody's Protest Art." *Antioch Review* 44 (Summer 1986): 261–275.

Eddy, Charmaine. "Material Difference and the Supplementary Body in Alice Walker's *The Color Purple*." *Body Matters: Feminism, Textuality, Corporeality*, edited by Avril Horner and Angela Keane, 97–108. Manchester and New York: Manchester University Press, 2000.

Evans, Mari, ed. *Black Women Writers (1950-1980): A Critical Evaluation*. Garden City, New York: Anchor-Doubleday, 1984.

Fifer, Elizabeth. "The Dialect and Letter of *The Color Purple*." In *Contemporary Women Writers: Narrative Strategies*, edited by Catherine

Rainwater and William J. Scheick. Lexington: University Press of Kentucky, 1985.

Gates, Henry Louis. Jr. Preface to *Alice Walker: Critical Perspectives Past and Present*, edited by Henry Louis Gates, Jr., and K. A. Appiah, IX–XIII. New York: Amistad, 1993.

———. "Color Me Zora: Alice Walker's (Re)Writing of the Speakerly Text." In *The Signifying Monkey: A Theory of African-American Criticism*, 239–258. New York, London: Oxford University Press, 1988.

Grimes, Dorothy G. "'Womanist Prose' and the Quest for Community in American Culture." *Journal of American Culture* 15, no. 2 (Summer 1992): 19–24.

Harris, Trudier. "Folklore in the Fiction of Alice Walker: A Perpetuation of Historical Literary Traditions." *Black American Literature Forum* 11 (1977): 3–8.

———. "On *The Color Purple*, Stereotypes and Silence." *Black American Literature Forum* 18 (1984): 155–61.

———. "Tiptoeing Through Taboo: Incest in 'The Child Who Favored Daughter.'" *Modern Fiction Studies* 28 (1982): 495–505.

———. "Violence in *The Third Life of Grange Copeland*." *CLA Journal* 19 (1975): 238–47.

Hite, Molly. *The Other Side of the Story: Structures and Strategies of Contemporary Feminist Narrative*. Ithaca, New York: Cornell University Press, 1989.

Holt, Patricia. Introduction to *Alice Walker Banned*. San Francisco: Aunt Lute Books, 1996.

Howard, Lillie P., ed. *Alice Walker and Zora Neale Hurston: The Common Bond*. Contributions in Afro-American and African Studies, no. 163. Westport, Connecticut & London: Greenwood Press, 1993.

Hudson-Weem, Clenora "The Tripartite Plight of African-American Women as Reflected in the Novels of Hurston and Walker." *Journal of Black Studies* 20 (December 1989): 192–207.

Johnson, Yvonne. *The Voice of African Women: The Use of Narrative and Authorial Voice in the Works of Harriet Jacobs, Zora Neale Hurston, and Alice Walker*. New York: Peter Lang Publishing, 1998.

Jump, Harriet Devine, ed. *Diverse Voices: Essays on Twentieth-Century Writers in English*. New York: St. Martin's Press, 1991.

Juneja, Om P. "The Purple Colour of Walker Women: Their Journey from Slavery to Liberation." *The Literary Criterion* 25 (1990): 66–76.

Lauret, Maria. *Alice Walker*. Modern Novelists, edited by Norman Page. New York: St. Martin's Press, 2000.

McDowell, Deborah E. "The Self in Bloom: Alice Walker's *Meridian*." *CLA Journal* 19 (1981): 262–75.

McGowen, Martha J. "Atonement and Release in Alice Walker's *Meridian*." *Critique* 23 (1981): 25–35.

Meese, Elizabeth A. "Defiance: The Body (of) Writing/ The Writing (of) Body." In *Crossing the Double-Cross: The Practice of Feminist Criticism*. Chapel Hill: University of North Carolina Press, 1986.

Montelaro, Janet J. *Producing a Womanist Text: The Maternal as Signifier in Alice Walker's The Color Purple*. English Literary Studies, edited by Samuel L. Macey, no. 70. Victoria: University of Victoria, 1996.

Petry, Alice Hall. "Alice Walker: The Achievement of Short Fiction." *Modern Language Studies* 19 (Winter 1989): 12–27.

Pickney, Darryl. "Black Victims, Black Villains." *The New York Review of Books* (January 29, 1987): 17–20.

Pryse, Marjorie. "Zora Neale Hurston, Alice Walker, and the Ancient Power of Black Women." In *Conjuring: Black Women, Fiction, and the Literary Tradition*, edited by Marjorie Pryse and Hortense Spillers, 1–24. Garden City, New York: Anchor-Doubleday, 1985.

Robinson, Daniel. "Problems in Form: Alice Walker's *The Color Purple*." *Notes on Contemporary Literature* 16 (January 1986): 2.

Selzer, Linda. "Race and Domesticity in *The Color Purple*." *African American Review* 29, no.1 (Spring 1995).

Shapiro, Laura. Rev. of *Possessing the Secret of Joy*, by Alice Walker. *Newsweek*, 8 June, 1992, 56–57.

Smith, Barbara. "The Souls of Black Women." *Ms.*, February 1974, 42–3, 78.

Smith, Dinitia. "Celie, You a Tree." In *Alice Walker: Critical Perspectives Past and Present*, edited by Henry Louis Gates, Jr., and K. A. Appiah, 19–21. New York: Amistad, 1993.

Stade, George. "Womanist Fiction and Male Characters." *Partisan Review* 52 (1985): 265–70.

Stein, Kara F. "Meridian: Alice Walker's Critique of Revolution." *Black American Literature Forum* 20 (1985): 382–92.

Steinem, Gloria. "Do You Know This Woman? She Knows You: A Profile on Alice Walker." *Ms*, June 1982, 35f.

Tate, Claudia. "Alice Walker." In *Black Women Writers at Work*, edited by Claudia Tate, 175–87. New York: Continuum, 1983.

Thielmann, Pia. "Alice Walker and the 'Man Question.'" In *Critical Essays on Alice Walker*, edited by Ikenna Dieke, 67–82. Contributions in Afro-American and African Studies, no189. Westport, Connecticut & London: Greenwood Press, 1999.

Thomas, H Nigel. "Walker's Grange Copeland as a Trickster Figure." *Obsidian II: Black Literature in Review* 6, no. 1 (Spring 1991): 60–72.

Walker, Melissa. *Down From the Mountaintop: Black Women's Novels in the Wake of the Civil Rights Movement, 1966-1989*. New Haven: Yale University Press, 1991.

Washington, Mary Helen. "An Essay on Alice Walker." In *Alice Walker: Critical Perspectives Past and Present*, edited by Henry Louis Gates, Jr. and K. A. Appiah, 37–49. New York: Amistad Press, 1993.

———. "I Sign My Mother's Name: Alice Walker, Dorothy West, Paule Marshall." *Mothering the Mind: Twelve Studies of Writers and Their Silent Partners*, edited by Ruth Perry and Martine Watson Brownley, 142–63. New York: Holmes & Meier, 1984.

Welsley, Richard. "Can Men Have It All? 'The Color Purple' Debate: Reading Between the Lines." *Ms.*, September 1986, 62, 90–92.

Whitaker, Charles. "Alice Walker: *The Color Purple* Author Confronts her Critics and Talks About Her Provocative New Book." *Ebony*, May 1992, 86–90.

Winchell, Donna Haisty. *Alice Walker*. Twayne's United States Authors Series, edited by Frank Day, no. 596. New York: Twayne Publishers, 1992.

Winchell, Mark Royden. "Fetching the Doctor: Shamanistic Housecalls in Alice Walker's 'Strong Horse Tea.'" *Mississippi Folklore Register* 25, no. 2 (Fall 1981): 97–101.

Watkins, Mel. "Sexism, Racism, and Black Women Writers." *The New York Times Book Review*, 15 June 1986, 1, 35–37.

Williams, Carolyn. "Trying to Do Without God': The Revision of Epistolary Address in *The Color Purple*." In *Writing the Female Voice: Essays on Epistolary Literature*, edited by Elizabeth Goldsmith. Boston: Northeastern University Press, 1989.

Contributors

HAROLD BLOOM is Sterling Professor of the Humanities at Yale University and Henry W. and Albert A. Berg Professor of English at the New York University Graduate School. He is the author of over 20 books, including *Shelly's Mythmaking* (1959), *The Visionary Company* (1961), *Blake's Apocalypse* (1963), *Yeats* (1970), *A Map of Misreading* (1975), *Kabbalah and Criticism* (1975), *Agon: Toward a Theory of Revisionism* (1982), *The American Religion* (1992), *The Western Canon* (1994), and *Omens of Millennium: The Gnosis of Angels, Dreams, and Resurrection* (1996). *The Anxiety of Influence* (1973) sets forth Professor Bloom's provocative theory of the literary relationships between the great writers and their predecessors. His most recent books include *Shakespeare: The Invention of the Human*, a 1998 National Book Award finalist, and *How to Read and Why*, which was published in 2000. In 1999, Professor Bloom received the prestigious American Academy of Arts and Letters Gold Medal for Criticism.

BRUCE and BECKY DUROST FISH are freelance editors and writers who live in Oregon. They have degrees in history and literature, and together they have written numerous books including several in titles in the Exploration of Africa book series.

HEATHER ALUMBAUGH is a Ph.D. candidate in English and American literature at New York University.

MARIA LAURET is professor of American Studies at the University of Sussex. She is the author of *Liberating Literature: Feminist Fiction in America* and *Alice Walker*.

HENRY LOUISE GATES, JR. is the W.E.B. Du Bois Professor of the Humanities, Chair of Afro-American Studies, and Director of the W.E.B. Du Bois Institute for Afro-American Research at Harvard University. His numerous publications include *Figures in Black: Words, Signs and the "Racial" Self; The Signifying Monkey: A Theory of Afro-American Literary Criticism*; and *Loose Canons: Notes on the Culture Wars*. Dr. Gates was awarded the American Book Award in 1989 for *The Signifying Monkey*.

Index